Shared Services in Finance and Accounting

Shared Services in Finance and Accounting

TOM OLAVI BANGEMANN

Routledge
Taylor & Francis Group

LONDON AND NEW YORK

First published 2005 by Gower Publishing

Published 2016 by Routledge
2 Park Square, Milton Park, Abingdon, Oxfordshire OX14 4RN
711 Third Avenue, New York, NY 10017, USA

First issued in paperback 2016

Routledge is an imprint of the Taylor & Francis Group, an informa business

British Library Cataloguing in Publication Data
Bangemann, Tom Olavi
    Shared services in finance and accounting
    1. Accounting 2. Managerial accounting 3. Shared services
    (Management)
    I. Title
    657

    ISBN 0 566 08607 7

Library of Congress Cataloging-in-Publication Data
Bangemann, Tom Olavi
    Shared services in finance and accounting / by Tom Olavi Bangemann.
       p. cm.
    ISBN: 0-566-08607-7
    1. Shared services (Management) 2. Accounting. 3. Business enterpises – Finance.
    I. Title.
    HD62.12.B36 2004
    658.4'02--dc22

                                                                    2004017868

Typeset by IML Typographers, Birkenhead, Merseyside

ISBN 13: 978-1-138-24761-1 (pbk)
ISBN 13: 978-0-566-08607-6 (hbk)

Contents

List of Figures

List of Tables

List of Abbreviations

ABC	acctivity based costing
AP	accounts payable
AR	accounts receivable
ASP	application service provider
BPO	business process outsourcing
BSC	Business Service Center
BU	business unit
CAO	chief administrative officer
CC	competence centre
CEO	chief executive officer
CFO	chief financial officer
CIO	chief information officer
CoA	Chart of Accounts
CRM	customer relationship management
CSF	critical success factor
CSS	customer satisfaction survey
EDI	electronic data interchange
ERP	enterprise resource planning
ERS	evaluated receipt settlement (in Europe: self-billing/self-invoicing)
EVA	economic value added (EVA is a registered trademark of Stern Stewart & Co.)
F&A	finance and accounting
FA	fixed assets
FAQ	frequently asked questions
FTE	full-time equivalent
G&A	general and administrative
GA	general accounting
GAAP	generally accepted accounting principles
GL	general ledger
GTA	German Tax Act (*Abgabenordnung*)
HR	human resources
IBC	integrated business center
IC	intercompany
IFRS	International Financial Reporting Standards (formerly IAS)
IRR	internal rate of return
IT	information technology

KPI	key performance indicator
M&A	mergers and acquisitions
MM	materials management
NAFTA	North American Free Trade Agreement
NPV	net present value
OCR	optical character recognition
OTC	order-to-cash
P&L	profit and loss (statement)
PERT	program evaluation and review technique
PMO	programme management office
PO	purchase order
PTP	purchase-to-pay
ROI	return on investment
SAP	service advertising protocol
SARBOX	Sarbanes-Oxley Act
SEC	Securities and Exchange Commission
SLA	service level agreement
SSC	shared service centre
SSO	shared service organization
T&E	travel and expense
TCO	total cost of ownership
TFC	training-focused centre
WTO	World Trade Organization

Acknowledgements

Thank you to Stewart Glendinning for helping to set the framework for the writing of this book, to William Foley for providing the US view and support and to Martin Wolleswinkel, Esther Schmid, Kai Zabel and Des Quinn for their review and content support, as well as to Christina Beck for help with formats and organization.

Thank you to all clients for their continued business relationships and trust, which have been a basis for the information necessary to put together this book.

Why Use Shared Services?

THE REVOLUTION

'A ghost is marching through Europe' was once the statement that described communism spreading around Europe. Some thought of the changes as a positive revolution; most feared them for being a threat to the known and appreciated status quo.

In finance and accounting organizations worldwide, a revolution is being carried out today. Due to the fact that few people in relation to the total population have any kind of relationship to a company's accounting work, it is not being widely noted and does not seem to be a ghost nor a danger, but the magnitude of this change is substantial and will be felt by most customers and consumers too. A new way of organizing back-office functions is being implemented across companies worldwide and finance is a front runner in taking this up. This finance revolution, called 'shared services', has taken over as the most discussed topic in finance in the last ten years and it will stay with us for some time to come.

Although the future is difficult to predict, it is useful to note some of the views found in the market place on future developments in this area:[1]

- Some say there will be only two types of companies in the future: those who outsource and those who do outsourcing.

- Others feel that all the work will disappear in the course of automation and only a small portion of exception handling will remain.

- Yet others think that virtual atomic corporations of the future will work in unconsolidated networks.

Certainly, the best way to predict the future is to invent it, but for those who prefer a more reactive approach, the future of shared services is a puzzle to be solved. This book is meant to serve as your guide to do just that.

THE BACKGROUND

There is hardly any company today that does not utilize shared services of some kind. This is also because the term 'shared services', originally defined by Greg Hackett, is

---

[1] All sources of information not specified are Answerthink and The Hackett Group.

today being used for a wide array of solutions ranging from tiny pieces of centralized work all the way to large global multifunctional offshore service centres. Some companies know they are using shared services, some don't – some call it that, some don't. In any case, we have long entered the maturity phase of shared services, so 'it will not go away'. The best thing now is to follow the saying: 'If you can't beat them, join them' and off you go with your own shared services project.

The reasons and drivers behind shared services, as with any new idea, are practical and pragmatic – as always in our economy. After entering the new millennium and finding the new economy had promised more than it delivered and recessive markets pushing everyone to their limits, companies found themselves solving the same issues they had been solving in the past, but with significantly more pressure to do so and to do so quickly. The results of their actions are what we read in newspapers every day:

- concentration on core business so that it is possible to grow horizontally and provide services or products on a more competitive basis
- increased speed in the globalization approach in order to act in a geographically wider market, possibly with global reach and coverage of developing markets
- acceleration of standard organic growth through acquired growth from mergers, acquisitions and divestments
- restructuring and re-engineering of both processes and organization occurring as permanent improvement cycles instead of exceptional projects
- people being described as the company's biggest asset, yet at the same time lay-offs increasing dramatically
- information technology (IT) budgets being scrapped, only to increase IT spending substantially in subsequent years as an acknowledgement of the company's total dependency on modern technology.

THE FINANCIAL SUPERHERO

All these developments, whatever triggers whatever else, have one thing in common: the chief financial officer (CFO) or finance head of a company must consider them and find answers and tools to react and act.

In addition to all the external pressures, CFOs have another nut to crack: internal dissatisfaction with the finance function. Several studies have proven that both employees inside the finance function and other partnering functions and internal customers rate the average finance function poorly in terms of:

- availability of the right skills inside the finance function
- optimal organization

- standardized, integrated systems

- decision-making data being flexible and accessible

- balance between routine and value-adding work

- availability of the right performance measures.

After all, the CFO has to satisfy several masters. The most prevalent issues include:

- How to provide excellent finance services for significantly less cost?

- How to be a value-adding business partner to other company functions?

- How to become a desirable place to work and attract external finance competency?

- How to deliver higher shareholder value?

The simple answer is to provide much more cost cutting, whereas what is actually required is to create a finance organization that adds more value to the business at a lower cost (see Figure 1).

Due to the restrictions on resources available in any organization, the major focus is on rebalancing the work. Increasing demands on business planning and risk

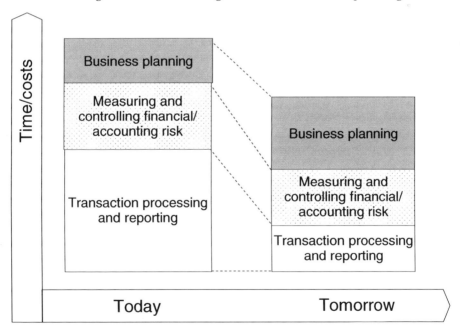

Figure 1 Creating a finance organization that 'adds more value at a lower cost'

management have to be met. The risk of not responding to these requirements is substantial and cannot be avoided. The only area to free up resources for this purpose is within the transactional finance area, including transaction processing and reporting. The activity pyramid that is standing on its head today, with most of the time spent on transactional activities instead of on strategic and more value-adding activities, has to be turned around and brought back to safe ground.

The CFO also has only a maximum of 24 hours available per day, so the increased attention required in the area of more value-adding activities is a critical issue. The finance function still needs to be managed but, more importantly, decision-support activities in defining new business models and dealing with investor relations, communication and value monitoring increase substantially in importance. Risk management increases also. The CFO is required to be a financial superhero capable of all these tasks (see Figure 2). As inside the finance area as a whole, the CFO too must free up resources by reducing time spent on transactional finance.

THE FINANCE FUNCTION OF THE FUTURE

The difficulty in setting up a finance function of the future that adds value at lower cost is that there are no silver-bullet answers as to how to do it. The trend clearly is to think more in corporate-wide finance competency than in the usual functional silos. 'What is needed in finance is a much greater leaning towards partnership, teamwork and involvement in the business' (source: Collum). Excellent finance, also, seems to lie in doing multiple things well – not just one thing at a best-practice level. Trends showing

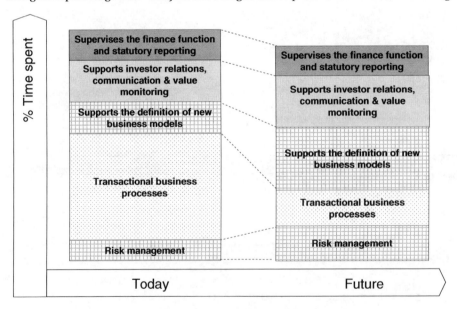

Figure 2   The CFO of the future is a 'financial superhero'

this are increased usage of statistically based, corporate-wide programs such as Six Sigma. However, with the current demand levels, all this translates into doing everything at a best-practice level or, in other words, being world class.

Now world class must mean doing everything at a best-practice level. The solution sought must be best practice in processes, IT, organization and so on and still fit into company strategy. Apart from making theoretical solutions thinkable, another look into the newspapers tells us that the major trend in solving the above issues is to install shared services. Why? Because a shared service organization (SSO) is the back office of the future and currently the only solution to all of the above issues.

THE TRUTH

There is no place here to focus on the discussion about dangers of globalization or whether 'concentration on core' is possibly just a trend. You could also discuss at length whether it is desirable from a socioeconomical point of view, and hence whether it should be allowed, that activities (and jobs) are moved from Western economies to lower labour cost areas such as India or China. Some US states and some European countries try to hinder this activity transfer using legal and regulatory means.

Let's stay pragmatic. The basic business truth for every company is that the main goal is to produce a profit and the main concern is the costs. It is useful, when looking at all the different reasons for shared services, benefits and dangers, approaches used and war stories told, not to get blurred and always to remember the basic facts, so as to guide you through the really important decisions on your way to a successful SSO.

Hence, we will stick to the facts throughout the book and base our views mainly on metrics and practical experience. The target is to provide substantial knowledge and subsequently decision support on four major questions:

- What are shared services?

- Are shared services the right answer for my company?

- How do I implement shared services?

- What comes after shared services?

PART I

The Basis for Shared Services

Even though the basic truth of having to produce a profit and manage costs is prevalent in most companies, more detailed and sophisticated analyses are necessary when calculating business cases and deciding on major organizational activities. As a result, reasons to go for an SSO or not to go do vary and the stated reasons vary too.

REASONS FOR SHARED SERVICES

Reasons for having a look at shared services can be external, internal and often are situational. Many transformations have been initiated because of major organizational trauma.

The company may desire certain outcomes, such as lower cost, reduction of risk or higher quality, or it may just want to use SSO as a change agent to push for an evolution of the mind-set inside the company. Later on in an SSO project, it is critical to know why shared services are initially implemented and what the goals are. It is useful to be honest in stating the goals, otherwise their fulfilment is endangered. Still, even if all participants are trying to be honest, goals can be conflicting and individual weightings of their importance can vary.

• Lower costs	• Improved customer service
• Higher quality	• Increased productivity
• Lower risk	• Economies of scale
• Standardized processes	• Improved controls
• Leveraged technology	• More timely and accurate
• Quicker decision making	information
• Improved focus on managing the business	• Supports mergers, acquisitions and divestments
• Encourages a 'one company' mindset	• Facilitates system migration

Figure 3   Shared services deliver value in a number of different ways

The top six reasons for an existing or planned finance SSO in the past are:

1. reduction in administration costs (80%)

2. grouping of similar tasks and expertise for a critical mass (62%)

3. improvement of services and quality, accuracy and timeliness (62%)

4. standardizing services (56%)

5. reduction in headcount and salary/wages (47%)

6. reduction in infrastructure costs (44%).

According to an ongoing global study by The Hackett Group (THG), 80% of companies name administrative cost savings as their primary reason for setting up shared services. This is clearly the main reason to go for SSO, although in previous years some studies showed quality reasons at the top of the list. In 2000 and 2001, the *Shared Services Study* by akris.com found quality improvements leading the list of drivers with 53% and 69% respectively (see Table 1 below).

Table 1 The four main reasons for setting up shared services

Reasons	2000 (%)	2001 (%)
Better service, improvement in quality accuracy, timeliness of information	69	53
Reduction of general administration costs	47	53
Standardization of services	15	48
Optimization of working capital*	–	42

* An issue in 2001

European results from 2003 for the first time show that cost aspects are again leading the list of deployment reasons. The picture otherwise is similar: there is a whole list of reasons to think about SSO.

It seems that companies in 2000 and 2001 were maybe not quite honest with their answers. From 2002 onwards, the difficult economic situation made it possible and necessary to state the truth: that costs had to come down. On the other hand, the conflicting interests in goals set for an SSO project can also result in misleading metrics. Many reasons might be important and often quality improvement goals are reasons that everyone is interested in. Also, productivity gains can be accepted by most as a reasonable goal, since these gains do not define as such where they come from. The sources could be reductions of full-time equivalent (FTE) but could also be new IT tools supporting higher-activity volumes per FTE. Cost reductions might be the

Table 2   Current top six reasons for an existing or planned finance SSO

Reduce administration costs	79%
Improve service and quality, accuracy and timeliness	69%
Reduce headcount and salary/wages	64%
Group similar tasks and expertise for a critical mass	61%
Standardize services	44%
Simplify roll-out and IT systems support	38%

single most important factor to really go for SSO, but this goal is not desirable for the majority of discussion participants as they fear negative personal effects. More detailed research by THG displays exactly this set-up: between 56% and 71% name customer service, quality and productivity as reasons for setting up shared services – only 32% name cost savings. However, the one single most important reason given is the cost savings (42%).

Table 3   Decision factors for the set-up of a finance SSO

	Important factor in the decision (%)	Single most important factor (%)
Process cost savings	32	42
Improved productivity	71	10
Improved process quality	61	5
Improved customer satisfaction	56	0

Note: Multiple answers possible

The US perspective is often criticized as being outweighed by global research. It is useful to look at reasons both for US and other regions, such as Europe, in order to get a feel for both current drivers and possible future reasons. Since shared services is a concept that was initiated in the US and then swapped over to Europe and other regions, some of the US reasoning can be seen in other regions after a time lag of some years.

Comparing the global results with European results, it is interesting to note that the reasons are actually very similar. In 2003, 79% of European-based companies stated cost reduction as the number one reason; in 2002 it was 80%.

A deeper look at these developments shows that most reasons have diminished in importance (see Table 4). Grouping similar tasks, reducing redundant tasks, standardizing services and reducing infrastructure costs are still named as important

Table 4   Reasons for setting up SSOs in Europe

	2002 (%)	2003 (%)
Reduce administration costs	80	79
Improve service and quality, accuracy and timeliness	62	69
Reduce headcount and salary/wages	47	64
Group similar tasks and expertise for a critical mass	69	61
Standardize services	56	44
Simplify roll-out and IT systems support	33	38
Reduce redundant tasks	42	36
Corporate strategy	40	35
Reduce infrastructure costs (premises, hardware, maintenance)	44	28
Enable flexible growth	33	19
Ability to serve a geographic area as a single market	6	15
Other cost savings	13	11
Improve working capital	–	11
As a temporary solution until non-critical company functions can be outsourced	9	3
Use of a Commissionare Model (shifting risks and returns to a more advantageous solution)	–	1
Other	7	–

reasons by a range of companies, but by much fewer than before. Overall administrative cost reduction was almost unchanged (79% and 80%) and headcount and salary reduction increased from 47% to 64%. It is obvious that wage cost reduction by volume reduction and wage arbitrage from relocating to low-cost locations are, next to quality issues, being considered the main drivers and have increased significantly in relation to other reasons.

Quality issues also have increased in importance in Europe and are the second most important reason. However, two different scenarios can be behind this. Some companies actually have a quality issue in terms of data not being consistent and reliable and not available on a timely basis. In other SSO projects quality is regarded something like a framework factor. The targets are set based on cost reduction and productivity gains. Existing quality is thought to be good or at least sufficient to fulfil compliance requirements and needs of customers and partners. Hence it is expected to improve cost and productivity within existing quality levels.

Other relevant reasons can be traced back to value-based thinking. Companies engaged heavily in M&A can support integration and enhance chances for synergy realization substantially by using an SSO as a platform. Since in general, most expected synergies are difficult to realize, an SSO can add value to a deal in the sense that administrative services do not need to be bought or at least can be integrated without significant costs. Since in M&A, prices are paid for products, customers, research knowledge, production facilities and so on, but not for the back-office finance activities, company values can be increased with an SSO that adds flexibility since administrative units do not need to be regarded a cost factor.

In the end, the decison to set up shared services almost always is a combination of many reasons. And even if the cost issue is a major one: 'An investment that changes our company is way too important to sit there and argue about cost savings.... We believe that this [shared service organization] is critical to the success of our company – and that's where we will go with it' (source: McMillan).

CASE EXAMPLE: Ford Motor Company

When Ford Motor Company 'invented' (together with General Electric) shared services in Europe in the early 1980s, it was more by accident than strategy. The story is that in Ford's Finnish subsidiary, a large group of finance people left the company at the same time. Hiring a group of new finance people that fast was not possible, so Ford was faced with practical problems in keeping up operations support, for example closing the books on time. A task force was set up, consisting of several Swedish finance people (Sweden being the nearest geographic location with available resources) supported by some other European employees.

At the end, the task force cleared the situation and it was found that it was possible to perform a major part of the finance activities for Finland from Sweden. Since Ford was reluctant to hire a whole new finance department, several activities were kept permanently in Sweden. Ford had successfully solved the practical resource issues and reduced both risk and cost for the future. Over time, this 'accidental solution' was found to work well and was implemented for other countries as well. About 20 years later, Ford moved the first finance process on a global basis to India.

CASE EXAMPLE: Hewlett-Packard

When Hewlett-Packard opened its shared service centre (SSC) in Brussels in the late 1980s, the main goal was to support the growth in new areas, for instance Eastern Europe. The goal was to be more flexible in delivering administrative services and avoid having to set up administrations for each new production or sales unit to be opened. As a result, the headcount of the SSC remained on a similar level for a long time, but continuous optimization enabled it to take over more and more volume. The opening and closing of entities and facilities was made easier. The real benefit therefore was not really in lowering existing costs, but in keeping costs at the current levels and, in a growth scenario, avoiding additional future costs that would have appeared in a traditional set-up.

CASE EXAMPLE: Henkel

Henkel started on its finance SSO journey in 1999. Apart from cost issues being a main driver, Henkel wanted to have more timely transparency about its financial performance and to support mind-set change towards a more European way of thinking. Organized into several very independent business units, sharing internal services and resources was not common in Henkel. Country organizations were run based on a decentralized culture and often the matrix organization included separate entities per business unit per country.

Henkel also realized that it was strongly involved in mergers and acquisitions, purchasing around 60–70 companies per year. A strong reason for a finance SSO was to find a way to support the successful integration of the purchased units. An SSO was a means to support Henkel's integration and possible divestments by being able to 'plug in and plug out' additional entities onto an integrated IT system by basically opening and closing new company codes.

DEFINITION OF SHARED SERVICES

Obviously there is a range of good reasons to go for an SSO. It is helpful now to know exactly what shared services are and what they are not. In reality, it is not important to stick to a specific wording or to engage in a theoretical argument about shared service definitions. However, it is important to have an agreed-upon vocabulary in any project or organization. All participants must understand what is meant when an SSO is discussed. It is advisable to restate the main definitions at the beginning of any such exercise.

Shared services can be defined in a number of ways. The definition depends largely on one's point of view. Some people feel that shared services are about organization; others think about processes. IT people would review the topic from their point of view. A chief executive officer (CEO) would think of the strategic fit of an SSO. Seven subject matters have to be taken into account when looking at shared services (see Table 5).

Table 5 Seven subject matters of an SSO set-up

Business strategy of the SSO	The business strategy with regard to strategic fit
Organizational concept	The decision on physical consolidation and the organizational alignment versus a virtual network
Process architecture	The core processes within the service centre and in the country organizations
Architecture applications	The ERP-specific subjects
Technological architecture and infrastructure	The infrastructure and technology within the service centre and the country organizations
Program and integration management	The consideration or integration of all projects within the company that are influenced by the shared service project
Personal question and change management	The answer to the personal question of each individual: 'What does that mean for me?'

As a result, a definition of shared services can focus on the reasoning behind it or the exercise to be mastered and result in, for example:

- an element of the company's strategy (perhaps for growth or to support concentration on core)
- an organizational restructuring
- a best-practice route
- a process re-engineering exercise
- a technology optimization project with organization and process alignment
- a mind-set change plan.

The definition could also focus more on the outcome, for instance on what type of organization the SSO will be:

● a world-class finance organization

● a professional services unit

● a low-cost administration services organization

● a valued business partner

● an integrated link in the value chain partnering with the business.

Surfing the Web will deliver hundreds more definitions. Often it is easiest to start with the organizational view (see Figure 4).

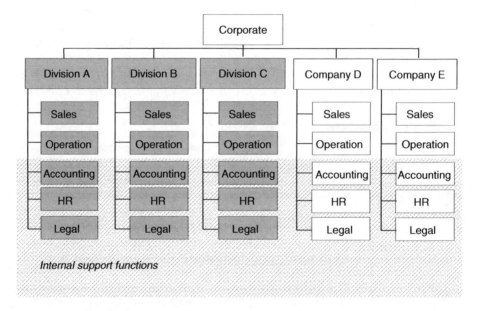

Figure 4   Typical organizational structure

In any company, the core business can be described as including one or many of the elements of sales, production, and research and development; in some cases it could include procurement activities. If you are not an accounting firm, then accounting will not be core. In a law firm legal advice is core but otherwise it is not. Any company can be described, in a simplified way, as consisting of core and non-core activities. The non-core activities include support functions, for example human resources (HR), procurement, IT and finance. Shared services focuses only on the support functions, not on core business or other operations.

The basic idea of shared services is simple. It copies what has been common practice in other parts of a company, an example being in production. Decades ago, companies would have produced a range of goods at the same production site to serve the market geographically located around that production site. Later, companies discovered that it made more sense to produce a limited number of goods in large volumes in one production facility and then to deliver to several markets. Shared services uses the same basic logic: provide services in one location to be used by several recipients in several other locations. Hence the name 'shared services', consisting of:

- *shared*: to be used by several recipients (internal customers, partners, businesses)

- *services*: focusing on services (internal and administrative, not operational outputs).

A unit providing internal services for just one customer is not a shared service, since there is no sharing amongst customers.

A service provider (as in 'shared services') has to be a professional service organization. The key here is the mind-set of the service's delivery people. An output is not in every case a service. A service has to do with serving, and requires the service provider to have the mind-set of wanting and needing to satisfy the (internal) customer. The difference to a standard back-office mentality can be evaluated with a list of criteria:

Yesterday:

Today (and for the future):

- net-income focused
- transactions processor
- reporting oriented
- functional
- demonstrating technical expertise
- law enforcer
- auditor
- information hoarder
- results driven.

- value-, cash-flow, and profit-focused
- insight provider
- planning oriented
- cross-functional
- demonstrating communication skills
- negotiator
- consultant
- information creator and sharer
- results and process driven.

Purely from an organizational point of view, the above standard organization chart, including an SSO, would look like Figure 5:

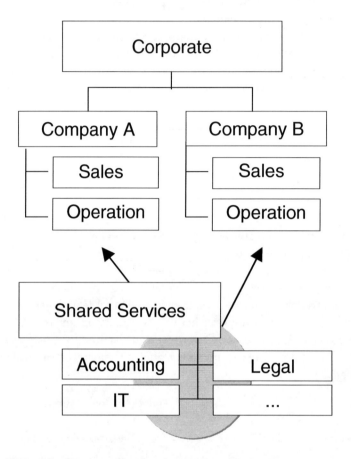

Figure 5   Shared services organizational structure

It would differ and differentiate itself from the standard organizational view mainly by three functional attributes:

- lower cost
- consistent timing
- reliable quality.

SHARED SERVICES VERSUS CENTRALIZATION

The problem with the organizational view is that even though we now understand shared services, the mind-set aspect is not reflected in the organization chart. Hence it looks similar to centralization. The consolidation of resources into one location also seems like centralization. It is useful to understand the differences between centralization and shared services:

Shared services:	Centralization:
● customer oriented	● focused on headquarters
● service is 'core business'	● 'support process'
● customer-specific services	● supplied service level
● ideal location (greenfield)	● headquarters as location (brownfield)
● full responsibility for cost and quality.	● low responsibility for costs and quality.

When the above five criteria for each definition are considered , the differences are obvious. It could also be said that shared services provide individual services and are hence demand oriented, whereas in centralized environments supply orientation defines outputs for everyone.

Yet, shared services are much more standardized, although the standardization reflects the standard processes – in other words the order of activities performed or the way things are done. In a standardized process it is still possible to produce different types of output, such as reports with different GAAP evaluations, invoices with different payment terms, fixed-asset bookings into different asset classes. There can be a range of payment methods from cash to direct debit, but the processes behind them should be standardized – in other words there should be only one way of performing direct debits (possibly with one bank). From a best-practice process-optimization point of view it makes sense to reduce the number of payment methods, but the number of payment methods does not define whether something is shared services or not.

The most visible selection criteria is the location of an SSC. Most companies would instinctively go for a central location near headquarters. Shared services, however, is based on selecting the most suited or ideal location. In most cases this would be a greenfield location, a location where the company has no presence.

In terms of cost responsibility, centralized back-offices do not have cost and quality responsibility whereas an SSO has full responsibility for what it does. It does not matter how this is linked to targets and measurements – whether the SSO is a cost centre, profit centre or separate legal entity – as long as it is one of these.

Alternatively, shared services can be looked upon as a combination of decentral-ization and centralization. An SSO combines the best of both worlds. It utilizes economies of scale from centralized approaches. It also recognizes local needs and leaves most decision power and control in the business units. Thereby an SSO actually supports a decentralized approach by freeing up local resources to concentrate on core operational activities. An SSO provides the platform to leverage economies of scale and to combine the critical mass of skills. Smaller local units often have a problem in attracting high potentials or sufficiently qualified finance resources. A professional SSO offers a finance environment that helps attract competent finance staff and thereby reduces risk and enhances quality.

SHARED SERVICES VERSUS OUTSOURCING

Shared services are sometimes described as 'internal outsourcing'. To differentiate from actual external outsourcing, the different forms of spin-offs or hive-offs can be described as embodying different solution types with the following standard versions:

- *Shared services*: establishing a separate internal service unit.

- *Joint venture*: establishing a separate internal service unit together with an external partner (to bring in expertise).

- *Outsourcing*: complete outsourcing to an external service operator.

The procedure to verify the feasibility is initially the same in all the cases and is conducted by a feasibility study (also called 'opportunity assessment' or 'business case') which will be explained in Part II.

A joint venture is a solution between (internal) shared services and (external) outsourcing. It is based on the thinking that for political or cultural reasons a company is not willing or able to move its finance operations completely to an outside provider. However, and possibly for the same reasons, the company does not trust its own know-how or ability actually to deliver the anticipated results. Hence, the company opts for a partnership with an external partner, who should deliver the know-how to carry out the optimization and manage the SSO. The majority of ownership is kept internal (for example 50% plus one share).

For the purpose of this book we summarize the definition of a shared service organization and a shared service centre thus:

A shared service organization (SSO)

- is an internal service organization, and
- consists of one or many shared service centres (SSCs).

A shared services centre (SSC)

- is a unit with consolidated, dedicated resources;
- provides process or knowledge-based services to several corporate entities;
- operates as a business within corporate structure;
- focuses on (internal) customers;
- uses contractual arrangements (service level agreements or SLAs) with its customers to define the service level.

The core elements of a shared services concept comprise:

- *Customer focus*: development of customer relationships internally and externally into business partnering
- *Cost leadership*: optimization of costs by keeping a balance between level of service and costs
- *Quality leadership*: delivery of highest quality possible through an organization that views services as its core business and makes them in perfect collaboration with its customers
- *Future outlook*: development of a sound and flexible basis for growth and change.

The key to Shared Services is treating what was once a corporate service like a whole new business. This is achieved by duplicating the environment of an independent service business, including customers, counting costs, and letting in the competition. Just as market competition improves a firm, so will it improve your in-house services (Source: JBS).

CHAPTER 1

Processes Covered by Shared Service Organizations

It is possible to decide, on a higher level, that a finance function as a whole should migrate into shared services. When actually preparing for the migration, it is necessary to take a process view on the scope. The whole shared services exercise is based on viewing the finance operations from a process point of view.

The process view is essential, because only this approach enables you to find out how different or how similar certain processes are. A company might be running an accounts payable (AP) process from one or many locations but that does not necessarily tell you how homogeneous the processes are. The homogeneity of a process or the potential to make it homogeneous is one of the key factors in finding out suitable processes for your SSO.

PROCESS DEFINITIONS

Processes develop into what they are over time. People working in those processes change the processes over time, mostly in order to optimize their own work effort. They change the order of activities they perform, they change the sources of information necessary for a task if a better source can be found, they set up new documents or new IT tools to help them. There is a variety of process types delivering essentially the same outcome, for example the creation of an invoice or the creation of a payment or a posting in the ledger. The order of activities to be performed to achieve each outcome can vary significantly.

This can be true even inside the same IT system. It is often not fully understood that an IT system does not guarantee a specific process and a system set-up is not the same as a process definition. A process consists of:

- activities performed by the process actor, for instance manual documentation or brain work
- verbal or technically supported communication between people
- usage of IT components in the process (e.g. input into the enterprise resource planning (ERP) system).

An IT system (such as ERP) sets boundaries inside which the process runs. The functionalities available in the system set something like a swim lane, inside which the process can move, consisting of manual activities, IT usage, communication, and so on. The system therefore guides the process into a certain direction but it does not guarantee a standardized process. Even with a fixed set of functionalities described as mandatory, the employees engaged could perform a set of activities in a different order, thereby changing the process. The exact degree of necessary standardization can be discussed, but a high degree is necessary for shared services to be performed efficiently. Since, in a standardized environment, individual activities are simpler and learned faster, the level of requirements as regards employees' skill levels decreases and makes lower-cost labour utilization possible.

Setting the process scope is one of the most interesting parts in SSO engagements. The selection of suitable processes needs to start with defining the processes. Not every company has been used to a process view and it might be unclear where a process starts and where it ends. For internal purposes in the first stage, a high-level split of activity clusters and their compilation into processes can be sufficient. At a later stage, more standardized process definitions will be necessary; for instance to benchmark the process performance with an external peer group. It is helpful to utilize process overviews and definitions available, an example of this being the finance process list from THG:

Transaction processing includes:

- accounts payable
- freight payments
- travel and expense
- fixed assets
- accounts receivable
- credit
- collections
- customer billing
- general accounting
- external reporting
- project accounting
- cost accounting
- cash management

- tax accounting
- tax filing and reporting.

Risk management involves:

- budgeting
- outlook/interim forecast
- business performance reporting
- treasury management
- tax planning
- internal audit
- government compliance
- tax regulatory.

Decision support:

- cost analysis
- business performance analysis
- new business and pricing
- strategic planning support
- finance function management.

Each process will have its content defined in detail. This is necessary for understanding where the links between processes are and for guaranteeing that there is no activity overlap in the definitions. An example from THG shows a possible process content:

Fixed assets: the process of recording and controlling the physical records and financial activities related to the assets of the company.

- Addition/verification of capital appropriation numbers to input documents.
- Verification/correction of capital spending captured in capital project tracking system.
- Collection of AP vouchers and other documentation required for asset set-up.
- Preparation of input documents for additions, deletions, transfers and adjustments.

- Data entry/keying into fixed-asset system.

- Reconciliation of fixed-asset system account balances and related constructed asset-clearing accounts to the general ledger (GL).

- Preparation of related journal entries.

- Distribution of fixed-asset reports.

- Record retention and preparation of asset folders.

- Development of fixed-asset accounting policies and procedures.

- Maintenance of depreciation tables and schedules for GAAP purposes.

- Development, training and support of inventory-tracking systems and procedures.

- Asset/inventory tagging.

- Conducting physical inventory of capital assets.

- Reconciliation of count-to-asset records, inventory records and GL.

- Management reporting specific to fixed assets.

- Audit support specific to fixed assets.

The hierarchy between processes, sub-processes, activities and so on can also be irritating. It is useful to agree on common terminology. No legal definition exists, but a useful hierarchy could look like that shown in Figure 6.

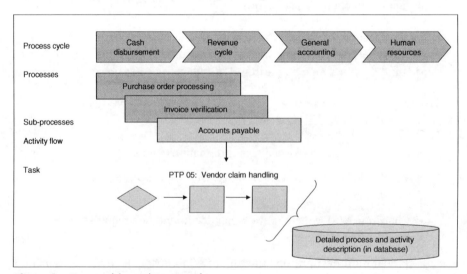

Figure 6   Process hierarchy example

Process cycles can have different names or different abbreviations. Choose the one which fits you best.

PROCESS SELECTION

The initial process selection can be made using a two-dimensional matrix based on two questions:

- *homogeneity*: is a process homogeneous in content and set-up or does it at least have the potential to be homogeneous?

- *strategy*: is a process strategic in importance – in other words, is it critical to strategic success and does it provide decision support?

Based on this matrix, processes with high homogeneity and low strategic relevance are those best suited for shared services. These are the transactional processes with high volumes, for example, AP or accounts receivable (AR). Processes with high strategic relevance and processes with low homogeneity need to be looked upon in more detail. They might be suitable or not.

Processes in the upper right corner of Figure 7 are strategically important and not homogeneous. An example could be the process of dealing with labour law issues. Certainly, labour law issues in most cases are a critical and very decision-relevant issue for any company. The issues can vary in type, risk effect, extent and so on, and are not homogeneous. In practice, a company could have one labour lawyer per entity. However, this would be inefficient because:

- not all entities have the same frequency of labour law issues and in the case of major issues a peak in lawyer resource utilization could not be covered by the individual entity, except if it held huge excess capacities all the time;

- a small legal department with one or few lawyers will not attract the best legal talent available resulting in lower skill levels available internally and the need to buy in external services.

In reality companies have solved this issue by consolidating several lawyers into one location or one organization; they then perform legal services for several companies. This is often called a 'competence centre' (CC) which is identical to the centre of expertise in Figure 7. A CC is also a type of shared service centre; however, the content is exactly opposite to that of a centre of scale. Also, a CC has totally different staffing requirements. It houses experienced experts who are expensive, performing processes with lots of variations. A centre of scale in its most extreme form would be a 'transaction factory' utilizing low-cost employees who perform standardized processes.

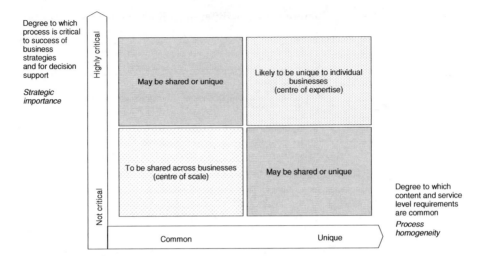

Figure 7   Process inclusion matrix

A centre of scale is what is normally referred to as an SSC. We will stick to this commonly used definition and use 'SSC' for the transactional shared service centre and 'competence centre' or CC for the centre of excellence. Both initially comprise the defined scope for a shared service organization but need to be separated and treated independently later. Areas in between a clear competency process and a clear transactional shared service process are the ones to be looked upon in detail before deciding.

Another way of looking at the process scope is to categorize it into core and non-core processes, based on the reasoning that core processes need to be invested in and non-core can be outsourced. This, however, will not lead to a lot of helpful results, as the finance processes are mostly completely non-core. The result would be to outsource everything, which can be an option but this initial selection would leave no room for more detailed analysis. It is helpful to enlarge this grouping to include:

● core processes

● essential processes (non-core but very important to management)

● non-core processes.

Table 6   Processes for shared services selection – finance and accounting

Core	Essential non-core	Non-core
Invest	Shared services	Outsourcing

Essential processes can include finance processes: processes clearly not core to the company, but regarded as essential and extremely critical by the management. Due to increased compliance issues in past years and increased legal activity to strengthen compliance (for example Sarbanes-Oxleyor SARBOX) certain non-core activities might still not be ready to be outsourced. These essential activities would be a category that could be executed from an SSO.

Naturally, the finance function is not completely essential either. Parts, such as mail room or travel and expenses (T&E) (if regarded as part of finance) could be outsourced on a local level. Other activities might be almost core, such as GL or parts of it, for example the final balance sheet review and 'optimization' activities performed including views and information from the highest company levels. Top management in any company would be reluctant to 'internally outsource' this activity to a service centre. The balance sheet set-up and its correctness are extremely important and many companies feel a need for it to stay close to top management. This activity, however, is in no way a core business of the company (except if it is an accounting firm). Hence, finance activities could be split into:

- activities performed locally
- activities performed in an SSO
- activities outsourced.

PROCESSES IN SSO

In reality, high-volume processes such as accounts payable (AP) and accounts receivable (AR) represent the top two processes being routed through SSO (see Table 7). This is not surprising, given that economies of scale are easiest to extract from high-volume processes. Both are bound to increase in usage in the next two to three years to up to 90%. This means that 90% of existing SSOs have AP in their scope in other words; AP is performed in the shared services centre(s).

Fixed assets (FA) ranks third and is very specific in having very high relative improvement potentials but is being rated less important by many companies due to low total FTEs involved. In most companies the fixed-asset ledger is not too complicated and is managed by one fixed-assets FTE or by someone performing the FA activities as part of his or her job utilizing less than one FTE for the fixed-assets work.

General ledger ranks fourth in popularity. In GL the percentage of activities transferred to an SSO, however, is lower (40–70%) than in accounts payable or accounts receivable, for example, which can be transferred almost completely.

Table 7   Actual utilization of processes in SSOs

	% of companies which have or will have implemented subsequent processes in their SSOs after expansion in 2–3 years	
	Today (%)	*2–3 years (%)*
Accounts payable	86	90
Fixed assets	74	80
Accounts receivable	76	80
General accounting	72	77
Travel and expense	66	71
Customer billing	59	67
Collections	64	64
Cash management	45	52
External reporting	45	46
Tax filing and reporting	41	45
Cost accounting	36	42
Credit	31	36
Freight out	29	28
Freight in	28	26
Order entry	14	19

Note: Multiple answers possible

Source: European Finance SSO Study 2003, The Hackett Group

Most processes have been increasing in the past years and will increase in utilization during the next two to three years. In recent years, there has been an increasing trend to include cost accounting in SSOs. Most of the cost accounting activities are actually on the competence centre side, not transactional. Still it makes sense to include them, but the trend seems to have levelled down. Freight (both incoming and outgoing) is on a relatively low level of utilization and is often either not relevant or in some cases is too complex to include. The trend is showing decreasing utilization.

General accounting (with an expected increase of 8% between 2003 and 2005) and cash management (with an increase of 7%) will experience the biggest increases in future years.

Credit, collections and customer billing are well suited for shared services. The reason for the relatively low utilization is that in many companies these processes are organized as the responsibility of the sales department or split between sales and finance. Although an SSO would support sales in concentrating on the selling, there is a reluctance on the side of sales to allow external customer contact to be performed by finance. This is based on the 'old view' of finance being a back-office team that does not know how to deal with customers. That might once have been true, but it is not true in an SSO, which is a professional service organization and could possibly perform even better than finance. As a result of this functional competency battle, the utilization of order-to-cash (OTC) processes especially has potential to increase.

Many companies launch an SSO with accounts payable, accounts receivable and components of general ledger as well as some of the other processes, mainly T&E and fixed assets, not only because they are mostly high-volume activities, but also because they satisfy the requirements to be good candidates for transferring to an SSO: the processes are homogeneous and act as support functions (they are not core processes which are vital to the overall business strategy).

Human resources processes are increasingly making their way into SSOs, in some cases into a cross-functional finance-based SSO. This makes perfect sense, since the only reason against that would be existing functional borders. A broader scope increases the influence of the SSOs to drive change and achieve superior results. The shared services trend that started with a few transactional finance processes is

Table 8 Shared service process selection pyramid

		Examples
Operating units	Decision support	Financial analysis Strategic planning Revenue enhancement Management of costs
Shared services	Reporting	General accounting Cost accounting Closing External reporting Management reporting Tax filing Reporting
	Transaction processing	Accounts payable Accounts receivable Billing Travel and expense Fixed assets

increasingly taking over more processes, also those which could be categorized as reporting or decision support.

The ability to split processes into activities, re-sort them and standardize makes it possible to include more and more processes in a transactional SSC. Also the IT developments, especially e-business tools, support the inclusion of more processes. In Table 8, the line separating processes to be performed locally from those in the SSC is moving upwards over time and has already reached a level in the middle of the reporting section. Hence, shared services in finance and accountancy have been primarily an issue of accountants but in future will affect also controllers more and more.

CHAPTER 2

The Location of Shared Service Organizations

Location, location, location! How often have we heard that phrase when it comes to selecting where we will live and work? One of the most critical decisions to be made during the formation of shared services is the determination of the location of the shared service organization and the individual shared service centres. According to a 2002 study (ACCA) 50% of companies view location as a critical success factor (CSF). A wrong decision can mean the difference between ultimate success and failure. There are no generic rights or wrongs; the decision comes down to what is right for the specific organization.

The location decision for shared services can often be driven by the need to be near existing company facilities ('brownfield site') as opposed to a completely new and independent location ('greenfield site'). The majority of companies start their location selection intuitively by thinking of their home country or even company headquarters. It is a thinking based more on centralization than on shared services. In shared services the optimal location should be the choice without regard to the proximity to headquarters. In reality, the optimal location can sometimes be the company's headquarters or home country, if political and tactical reasoning is of major importance. Changing the location thinking is a change process that needs to build on a thorough understanding of what an SSO is and what it can perform despite possible geographical distance.

Recent research on proximity issues shows that:

- 46% of SSCs purposely desire proximity to corporate headquarters
- 68% of SSCs believe it critical to locate close to existing company operations (non-headquarters)
- 57% of SSCs wanted to locate near existing company employees.

Interestingly, practical experience with location choices of companies who have set up SSOs lets us conclude that most companies who chose 'greenfield' sites viewed their implementations as extremely successful or very successful, while maybe half of those co-locating with other company facilities felt the proximity had negative effects on performance.

The location decision for shared services goes well beyond the analysis of costs and skilled labour. One can only conclude that the company's internal political environment also factors into this decision. Therefore, the 'serious and fact-based' location decision provides the opportunity to overcome some of the common opinions about SSO in general that may exist:

- 'Creating shared service centres is another attempt by corporate headquarters to take away the autonomy of the business units and expand their bureaucracy.'

- 'A shared services centre is basically a "transaction sweatshop" that is unable to attract quality employees and offer them an attractive future.'

- 'Decentralized administrative support functions are more effective because they are closer to the customer.'

- 'Any minor efficiencies gained in migrating to shared services will never offset the high start-up costs.'

It is important to ensure that shared service leaders are not 'sucked into' a political debate on where to locate. In the example of a pharmaceutical company, the location analysis provided a shortlist including locations such as Barcelona, Dublin and Maastricht. The discussion took months to explain to some top managers that their current job sites (for example Berlin and Paris) were not competitive. The company then, having worked out this list, felt that the location choice should consider an additional criterion which was something like 'general split of work and overall buy-in and satisfaction'. The company concluded that France and Germany had profited from certain operational location decisions and hence the UK should house the SSC, because the UK was their third largest market in Europe. In another location discussion, the company management suggested places like Nice and Marbella as potential candidates for the long list. Naturally these locations too can be analysed but the selection criteria need to be clarified early in the process.

The selection of a site for a shared service centre can be a challenging and complex exercise for any company. Due to the critical nature and long-lasting impact of this decision, the company must carefully weigh all the relevant factors in order to make the most beneficial choice of location. A transparent and analytical approach is best suited to this.

NORTH AMERICA

In North America in general, the locations selected are easier to choose (compared to other parts of the world) based on a list of optimal location criteria, since inside one country or one economic zone (such as the North American Free Trade Agreement or NAFTA) language and legal issues are less pressing and labour law is more flexible and allows relocations more easily.

In North America, businesses often prefer to locate the new shared service centres away from the bureaucracy and unresponsiveness of corporate headquarters. However, as indicated above, 46% of the Hackett survey respondents suggest that the availability of facilities, ready-trained staff and often corporate politics dictate the location of shared services near an existing company facility. Proximity to an existing company operation can also foster good customer service, aid communication and offer shared service employees a career path into business operations.

Unlike Europe and Asia, where local language and legal issues are critical to the location decision, in North America the objectives of this decision are mainly based on the opportunity the location provides to drive the lowest total cost of ownership while providing high levels of service and quality. An objective, and thorough, analysis is important to gain acceptance in the organization and to build momentum for the change process. While not intended to be comprehensive, the following represent some of the key selection criteria involved in this decision:

- total cost of ownership

- risk mitigation

- business supportability

- speed to implementation

- intangibles.

We will have a detailed look and try to further understand the importance of each of these key selection criteria and some of the details which comprise them in Part II of this book when dealing with the location analysis.

In the United States, there is one primary business language and one currency. The vast majority of shared service site-selection decisions result in a site being selected in the proximity of corporate headquarters or near a business unit. Achievement of a business-case objective is the primary driver. An emerging driver in the site-selection decision (as well as the scoping decision) for shared services is compliance with Sarbanes-Oxley controls. This legislation has become another reason why US companies have opted to keep their shared services near their corporate or business-unit locations. However, locating the shared service centre in suburban areas has benefits ('B' or 'C' grade real-estate facilities as opposed to 'A' space in city-centre locations).

In terms of actual results of the location selection, there does not seem to be one clear winner in terms of one city or region that beats everybody else. Unlike Europe, Asia and for that matter Latin America, there is no clear concentration in the US of a huge number of SSCs in one geographical area. Despite the lack of a clear favourite and the fact that it really comes down to the individual company's business case, we can conclude from realized SSO projects that for US companies it is interesting to have a look at locations in southern or south-western cities (for instance in Florida, New Mexico, Oklahoma) because of their relative cost advantage compared to the north or north-east.

Canadian locations often have cost advantages of approximately 20% based on the wage difference and there are currently (and possibly in future) some reasons for US companies to consider Canada due to the favourable exchange rate (Canadian dollar to US dollar). Employees are well skilled and knowledgeable of US GAAP; many speak multiple languages and have a good work ethic. Social-security issues can potentially be a constraint and may prevent centres from being able to downsize their high-cost employee base with a high cost. Companies like Lafarge Construction Materials, BP North America, Holcim, and Procter & Gamble, amongst others, have located their North American service centres in Canada.

Mexican locations can offer even bigger savings potentials and hence locations like the Mequilla Dora region, Monterrey and Guadalajara are very popular as SSC locations. Mexico has the advantage over other Central American countries in that it is part of NAFTA, but barriers in terms of language and US GAAP knowledge (given the Sarbanes-Oxley legislation) make a move to this region somewhat limiting. Nevertheless, Central American locations are increasingly winning over SSCs, exhibited for example by the set-up of an SSC of Procter & Gamble in Costa Rica. A potential free trade agreement including both Americas would certainly boost Latin America's chances as a location choice for US companies.

This is especially true for those centres previously located in Florida (especially the Miami area) as 'Latin American' centres could lead to their relocation. Mexico has been viewed as popular mainly because of the low cost of labour. US companies looked eagerly at the opportunity to move their shared services to Mexico to reap the benefits of the labour cost differential. Mexico has been considered by US companies to serve their Latin American operations; however, turnover can be high and the total cost offers limited advantage.

Shared services based in Mexico serving North America include Lufthansa (serving their North and South American operations), HP (global information technology), Telefonica (also serving their North and South American operations) and Cummins (serving their Latin American locations).

EUROPE

In Europe, the majority of European companies (51%) have SSCs within their home country, representing 35% of all their SSCs. These 51% are a radical decrease from 86% in 2002. The practice of establishing locations in other European countries has increased from 55% in 2002 to 64% in 2003 and is projected to increase to 97% by 2006. This means that almost all companies plan to set up (one of) their SSCs in a European country other than their home country.

Table 9 Geographical roll-out of European-based SSOs

	Today (%)	2–3 years (%)
Home country	51	64
Other countries in Eastern Europe	26	36
Other countries in Central/Western Europe	38	61
Middle East/Africa	1	3
NAFTA	14	18
South America	8	14
Asia-Pacific	8	14

Note: Multiple answers possible

Table 10 Greenfield versus brownfield location

Greenfield (at a different new location)	17%
Brownfield (at another existing location where you have operations)	53%
At headquarters	48%

Note: Multiple answers possible

For European companies, proximity to corporate headquarters and to existing operations is a significant factor in location decisions, even if in specific cases the opposite holds true. These exceptions are cases where change of corporate culture, abolishment of existing union contracts or other special circumstances (for example merger situation) give rise to a different set of selection criteria. Hence 51% choose to locate in their home country, 26% are willing to locate in another European country. In total, just 17% prefer greenfield locations – locations with no existing operations before the SSO. This shows that the 'optimal location' selection is still influenced heavily by centralization thinking and political and legal aspects.

The initial trend in Europe in terms of choosing a location outside the home country was at the end of the 1980s and during the 1990s to go to Ireland. The Republic of Ireland offered relatively inexpensive young labour resources (due to high unemployment) and tax incentives to attract relocation into Ireland. Hundreds of call centres opened in Ireland and were soon followed by finance SSCs. A screening of countries and cities was performed by many companies resulting in the common practice of performing a location analysis before choosing a location. Such a location analysis would select a location based on a list of criteria weighted by the individual company based on its targets and preferences (see Part II).

After the boom in locating in Ireland, which in terms of cities then was mainly Dublin and today includes Cork, there were several other interesting locations appearing on location analysis lists. The UK was able to offer a range of competitive locations especially in Wales, Scotland and the Midlands including Manchester, Chester, Liverpool, Newcastle, Cardiff and Glasgow. Even London attracted a range of SSCs based mainly on the wide language and skill availability and less on the cost advantages.

Benelux as a region was a competitive solution, especially in the 1990s. Brussels won several location contests due to its cosmopolitan workforce, which is mainly a result of EU institutions being located in Brussels. Many of the SSCs in Brussels employed spouses and family members of EU representatives. Other locations outside but near Brussels followed, being able to offer almost the same accessibility and lower costs. Several Dutch locations, including Amsterdam, Rotterdam and Maastricht, were location choices based on a good mix of an affordable workforce and good skill sets. Also, the geographic location of the Netherlands offered a central point in Europe easily reached from many European countries. Because of the relatively small size of its economy, it was also politically a good compromise when fighting between the large subsidiaries of a corporation in Germany, UK and France could not be decided.

After the trends to locate SSCs in the British Isles and Benelux, the next big wave went south to Iberia: Portugal and especially Spain. In Spain, Madrid and more often Barcelona were preferred locations. Barcelona is known for housing SSCs including those from General Motors, Hewlett-Packard and Bayer, and was a preferred location mainly due to a favourable mix based on inexpensive labour costs but also offering an improved infrastructure, accessibility and in general a living environment regarded as attractive. SSCs in Barcelona often started with a small selection of transactional finance processes and were later enlarged.

At the time of writing, the current trend is towards Eastern European countries. Although other locations remain strong location choices, Eastern Europe shows the largest increases in SSCs. Of the companies deciding to locate outside their home country, those in the UK lead with 9% of SSCs being located there, followed by businesses in Spain (8%) and Poland (7%). In Poland, Warsaw and Krakow are particularly popular locations. Southern cities in Poland are preferred when SSCs require a workforce with a high degree of German language capability readily available. Prague in the Czech Republic and Budapest in Hungary are the other two leading location choices in Central/Eastern Europe. Budapest houses SSCs from Diageo, IBM and Alcoa, amongst others.

In many cases, location decisions are based on existing SSO operations from other companies; in other words, there is a tendency for companies to follow others' lead. The first companies that moved into Dublin, for instance, created the infrastructure, trained the people and demonstrated success. Others then followed. A similar trend occurred in the UK where there is a clustering of SSCs in certain regions. The best location for SSCs in Eastern Europe too will probably be where some large SSCs have just set up and are demonstrating that the infrastructure works.

Scandinavia as a region also attracts a fair amount of SSCs, especially when companies go for a regional approach. Copenhagen in Denmark and several Swedish sites are the strongest contenders here.

Table 11   Preferred countries for a European SSC

SSC locations selected by companies locating outside their home country	
Central Europe	17%
British Isles	15%
Iberia	12%
Scandinavia	4%
Eastern Europe	15%
Other European countries	13%
Asia	8%
NAFTA	10%
South America	6%

Source: European Finance SSO Study 2003, The Hackett Group

There is a number of companies choosing to set up SSCs in Germany, France, Switzerland and Italy, but almost without exception these are not pan-European SSCs, and, if they are, then that is the home country of the company in question.

Twenty-two per cent of European companies prefer (additional) locations outside Europe. In most cases these are used for SSO coverage in that region or to set up a global SSO.

OTHER REGIONS

South American SSC activity has increased substantially in the last few years. Regional SSCs for South America work especially well. There are few companies considering global or cross-regional activities to be performed from South America, maybe with the exception of some Spanish companies relying on strong historical and language ties working in their favour. In terms of location choice for the regional SSCs, Chile has been preferred as location choice more often than other countries (by Unilever and Beiersdorf, for example) but certainly Brazil and Argentina are also locations to consider.

Africa is a bit of a white spot on the location map. South Africa is an exception, but it houses mainly national SSCs. North African countries, such as Morocco and Egypt, are becoming more interesting as location choices. Some countries like Ghana and Mauritius house existing SSCs, some of them run by business process outsourcing (BPOs).

Asia and the Asia-Pacific region are currently front runners in SSCs. Countries like India and the Philippines have been popular locations for some years. India is known to be a particularly strong BPO site and offers almost unbeatable labour costs. Salaries can be up to 80–90% below Western levels. This enables companies to compensate for possible inefficiencies. Originally the infrastructure (facilities, telecoms and so on) was an issue but today's conditions are competitive. A range of SSCs, mostly outsourced, are operating from Bangalore or Delhi. Over the past few years, many UK call centres have also relocated to India; these include British Airways, British Telecom, Finance companies (such as AXA and Abbey) and banks (for example Barclay's and Lloyds TSB). This trend is likely to continue.

The rising star in Asia in terms of shared service locations is China. There is a range of SSCs today in China, especially in Hong Kong, Shenzen, Guangzhou and Shanghai. Since the entry of China into the World Trade Organization (WTO) in 2003, it can be expected that the country's legal and regulatory environment will improve. The labour costs in China can be lower than those in India and labour availability is currently good, catapulting China into a position of probably becoming the preferred site for SSCs in the future. The main issue, apart from regulatory complexity, is the sufficient foreign language efficiency and the difficulty in finding (measured by Western standards) a more experienced workforce.

Australia and New Zealand house a range of SSCs, mostly with national or regional coverage. Companies based in Australia and New Zealand have been quite early and active movers in terms of shared services, but these countries are not a preferred location for global activities or from a European or North American point of view. Asian countries such as India would, if the distance is acceptable in general, then be the better choice in most cases.

CHAPTER 3

Benefits and Obstacles to Setting Up a Shared Service Organization

USAGE OF SHARED SERVICE ORGANIZATIONS FOR FINANCE

The majority (71%) of European companies today have at least one SSO implemented for the finance function. This is up significantly from 54% in 2002. Another 16% of European companies are planning to implement a shared service organisation within the next two to three years. The shared services concept has hence definitely made its breakthrough in Europe. Most companies though are still in 'project mode' with 40% of all companies and 55% of those with an SSO planning an expansion of their SSO, while only 13% stated that their scope, in terms of processes and countries in their SSO, was complete.

Table 12   European finance SSO utilization

Companies *currently operating* a finance SSO	71%
Companies planning a finance SSO *within the next 2–3 years*	16%
Companies *not planning* a finance SSO	13%

An 'expansion' means that additional geographical locations will be introduced and/or more finance processes will be moved to an SSO. An expansion is quite normal due to the approach that companies choose to implement shared services. They often go stepwise or in a phased approach; in other words, they start with a certain scope and enlarge it later, if successful. The number of completed SSOs does not seem to grow as companies are mostly successful and keep enlarging their scope. Whatever the reasons, for more than half (58%) of the companies with an SSO, the experience with a shared service organization has been so good that it is driving an expansion. Out of the 29% that do not have an SSO yet, 55% plan to introduce it in the next two to three years. Europe-based companies have rapidly increased their utilization of shared services and thus gained valuable experience in extracting their potential benefits. They still lag behind US companies in terms of years of experience and average cost levels, but utilization levels have equalized.

FINANCE COST OVERVIEW

Cost levels are measured by a range of different key performance indicators (KPIs). Most commonly the cost aspect is measured using the overview KPI of finance cost as percentage of revenue. Based on this KPI, North America is significantly more cost effective than other regions. However, world-class companies from Europe have closed the gap with their North American peers.

Table 13   Finance cost as a percentage of revenue: selected regional comparisons

	Average (%)	World class (%)	Difference (%)
North America	1.01	0.54	-45
Europe	1.27	0.54	-57
Latin America	1.58	0.97	-39
Asia-Pacific	1.22	0.68	-44

A comparison of European companies' finance costs with global average figures makes it clear that European companies have improved their performance from 2000 to 2002 by nearly 20% but still have a gap of almost 20% to close.

Table 14   European finance costs versus worldwide finance cost

	2000	2002
Europe finance cost (%)	1.58	1.27
Worldwide finance cost (%)	1.05	1.06

It is important to remember that one KPI can never tell the full story, but it can be a useful starting point in looking at the cost drivers and detecting improvement potentials. It is remarkable, however, how this one KPI can be tracked over the past ten years and how it exhibits the story of optimizing the finance function very well, delivering the metrical proof for the results gained.

Table 15   Ten-year development of finance cost as a percentage of revenue

	1992	1994	1996	1998	2000	2002
Average (%)	1.90	1.70	1.50	1.52	1.20	1.10
World class (%)	1.50	1.26	1.10	0.98	1.00	0.72

The drivers behind this continuous improvement have been the same throughout the whole period. Even though many of the underlying optimization programs had nothing to do with SSOs at the time, the drivers from today's point of view look almost identical:

- process simplification and standardization

- leverage of new technology

- realignment of the organization.

In terms of SSCs' experience in serving several countries and encountering different regulatory and cultural environments from one SSC, Europeans are now clearly ahead, as most North American SSCs are national in scope. On the positive side, this gives both European and US companies a range of reasons to intensify the exchange of learning experiences with each other.

REASONS FOR DEPLOYMENT OF SSOs AND BENEFITS ACHIEVED

Benefits achieved can be looked at separately or in comparison to the set targets or reasons for deployment. We make reference to the discussion about reasons in the Introduction to this book.

Fully 80% of global and 79% of European companies trace their decision to implement an SSO to a desire to reduce costs. This is almost unchanged from previous years. For European companies improvements in service and quality have become the second most important factor (69% – up from 62% the previous year). This is the logical result of quality issues (52%) and IT issues (47%) being the largest stumbling blocks when implementing an SSO. It seems that many companies have set up possibly too progressive implementation plans and as a result of this in the course of the project experienced quality problems in operations and business partnering with the IT function.

Reduction of personnel and related cost, for instance by leveraging lower salary and wage rates, has increased significantly from 47% to 64%. This is clearly an outcome of the general economic climate creating increased cost pressure and possibly from stating goals more honestly and precisely. These results are in line with detailed findings of The Hackett Group on global shared services, where cost savings are mentioned by 32% of companies as an important factor but by 42% as the single most important decision factor. Other factors mentioned as important rate higher, for example improvement in productivity (71%), improvement in process quality (61%)

and customer satisfaction (56%), but at 10% or lower in score in terms of being the single most important factor, all these factors are rated not decisive.

COST OPTIMIZATION POTENTIAL

Obviously the experience with optimizing the finance function is positive and the driving factors are benefits that can be gained from an SSO, so the type and magnitude of those benefits to be gained are a major point of interest to be discussed in more detail. It is interesting to note that the potential in optimizing the finance function is huge but, relative to some other support functions, it is rather small. Comparing 'good' and 'bad' performers in four support areas shows how large the range actually is. There are huge differences between world-class companies and 'normal' performers but also between average and 'bad' companies.

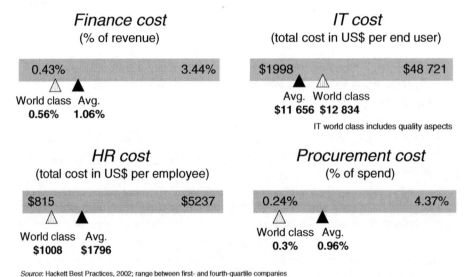

Source: Hackett Best Practices, 2002; range between first- and fourth-quartile companies

Figure 8   Overview of cost for finance, IT, HR and procurement

In finance, this gap between first- and fourth-quartile companies can be ten times the cost or even more. However, in IT or procurement this gap is even higher, sometimes 20 times the cost or more. Also, the absolute cost potentials are often higher in other support functions, so benefits should be relatively easier to gain. In reality, finance has the benefit of processes that are quite well suited for SSOs and hence has been driving this change more than the other functions.

And the potentials are still huge. On an individual process level, for instance payables, there is more than a ten-fold cost difference between good and bad performers. In payroll (sometimes looked upon as HR, sometimes categorized as a finance process) the difference is 'only 5x', but based on these differences in performance, the potentials for companies that are not performing well are absolutely marvellous.

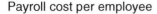

Payroll cost per employee   Payables cost per line item

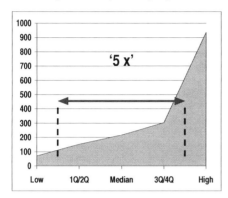
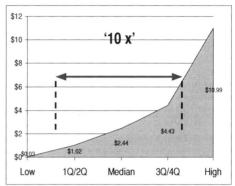

Figure 9   Cost gap overview: payroll and AP

COST BENEFITS

When discussing cost savings, definitions are good to mention. Cost benefits in SSO are often measured by run rate savings: the difference of annual operational cost between the situation before and after SSO. A company could have had finance costs of one million per year and in the SSO environment has annual costs of 800 000. That would be a 20% saving in terms of a continuous saving applicable for every year – the fixed cost of running the finance function is 20% lower than before.

Results from implementing an SSO in terms of savings are very positive and support the validity of how business cases performed in the feasibility study. Realized savings are almost identical to planned savings. Forty per cent of European companies have savings of 21% or more; another 40% have savings of 11 to 20%. In total that is 80% of European companies with an SSO with savings of 11% or more.

Table 16   Planned versus realized savings from SSO

	Over 2% cost increase	*2% cost increase to 10% cost reduction*	*11–20%*	*21–40%*	*41–80%*
Planned	0%	14%	40%	32%	14%
Realized	0%	19%	40%	26%	14%

By way of comparison, 64% of participants in The Hackett Group's ongoing global shared services benchmark have achieved reductions of at least 11% in transaction costs, with 37% of the participants achieving a minimum cost reduction of 21% (see Table 17). The latest European results for the first time are better that those of their US peers. However, there are several important things to consider in terms of these figures.

Table 17   Cost savings from SSO (over time)

41–80% decrease	23%
21–40% decrease	14%
11–20% decrease	27%
2% increase – 10% decrease	23%
+2% increase	13%

US-based companies have achieved relatively high savings. Twenty-three per cent of companies globally (including mostly US companies) report savings of 41 to 80%. This is often based on their advantage of having started earlier. In the set-up of shared services, companies move in phases. These companies have been able to increase their scope over time, so that they have now reached a critical mass that makes these results possible. Also, these results are often gained in cases where:

- the previous performance was very bad, so the performance potential was huge;

- the SSCs are located in low-cost locations which provide significant financial benefits, even if no productivity improvement has taken place;

- US companies have been more aggressive and successful in implementing single ERP platforms globally which have given the SSOs additional improvement potential.

It is very important to look at savings and interpret them in relation to:

- what the starting position (performance) was;

- where savings come from (productivity gain, wage arbitrage from location change and so on).

It is useful to discuss savings with other companies in a collaborative environment, but it is not useful to discuss their savings with several other finance heads, then pick the one with the highest figure and assume that their approach must have been the best. The opposite could actually be the case.

The above results also exhibit that globally 13% of companies have not reached cost savings or have actually higher costs today than before. This could be due to three main reasons:

- The project was not successful.

- There were no savings goals (the project was performed for quality, transparency, risk reduction or other reasons).

- The project does have savings goals, but is in such an early stage that they have not yet been realized and project costs are blurring the picture.

Some of the SSO projects are not successful. In some cases an SSO does not make sense. This is why a feasibility study is a useful exercise to go through before a company jumps into the design and implementation of an SSO. Some practical examples of companies that were not successful failed for the following reasons:

- The business case was not set up or was set up incorrectly and hence the company engaged in a project that could not deliver the anticipated results.

- Change management effort and internal resistance to it were underestimated and the project could not be implemented successfully; perhaps critical mass was not reached because several units did not participate or the SSO was set up but other functions blocked the performance.

- The SSO was set up in parallel to other projects which had competing targets (for instance, the commissionaire model did not match process optimization targets) or different projects were not linked together (perhaps an IT platform was being developed independently of the SSO).

In one case, a US$1 billion revenue company had about 30 units across almost all European countries as well as in the Near East and in the Caucasian countries which it tried to integrate into one SSC. The company set up shared services with one ERP platform and standardized processes. Nevertheless, the project was not successful and the SSC was dismantled. This might have been because most units had very small finance departments with between one and five FTEs. Several countries in which they operated had a difficult regulatory environment. It was not possible to generate benefits due mainly to missing volume in these locations and their diverse regulatory workload. A regional approach leaving out of scope some of the very small but difficult countries might have worked, but once an SSO fails it will be some time until it will be given another try.

There is a range of other possible reasons for failure that we highlight further below when discussing critical success factors and risks.

Some SSO implementations do not have savings goals. As mentioned in the Introduction, there can be a range of other reasons to set up an SSO. In the end, the goal is to support the business for it to produce better products, sell more and deliver overall better results for the company. Therefore, the goal is not necessarily to reduce headcount or even cost, but to be in a better position to support the business. This could result in, for example, an SSO to support future growth by having a faster and more flexible support organization or an SSO with improved quality and better utilization of potentials than an IT system can provide. Actually these other benefits will deliver cost savings in the sense of avoided costs. Costs, for example for setting up new administrations for newly opened subsidiaries or plants, can be avoided by supporting them from an existing SSO. Therefore, the pure fact that 13% of companies did not report cost savings is not necessarily an indication of failure. Neither is the fact that 10–20% are regarded as insufficient by some companies. The estimated savings (by companies themselves) show that such figures are contingent on the status of the project. In 1999 only 6% globally had savings of 20% and more (according to akris).

Future savings are estimated to be higher, mainly because SSO projects will advance to the next phase and reach critical mass and higher volumes. Internal centre optimization needs time and will also improve results, as well as the new IT platforms that are put in place.

Table 18   Anticipated cost savings from SSO (over time)

	Hackett Global Finance SSO, 2005 (estimated)
41–80% decrease	23%
21–40% decrease	29%
11–20% decrease	20%
2% increase – 10% decrease	16%
+2% increase	12%

Companies with SSO versus companies without SSO

Since the validity of benchmarking results is mainly dependent on the apples-to-apples comparison, it is necessary to compare good companies with good companies and bad performers with bad performers, if we want to find out about the difference between performance in companies with and without SSO. A comparison of companies globally with and without SSO, with both making up about half the database, makes the cost benefits of SSO extremely transparent (see Figure 10).

Table 22   SSO's estimated impact on overall productivity

	% of centres	
	To date (%)	In 3 years (%)
Greater than 2% decrease	4	2
0% +/- 2% impact	5	2
3–10% increase	25	9
11–20% increase	34	34
Greater than 20% increase	32	53

important to know how different persons perform against each other; just how the department or the overall process performance looks and how activities as a whole are performed. In some cases measurement will be at the individual level, as there might only be one person performing a certain activity or process. In order to comply with data protection legislation that is in force in almost all countries (even if very different in strength) it is good to check the measurement methodology when starting. From an IT point of view, today almost any measurement, even individual, is possible. In some cases companies have stated that the ability to track individual performance was a significant location selection reason. Depending on the culture or cultural targets, it might be necessary or desirable to be able to openly discuss performance with individuals and groups, for instance in weekly team meetings with performance figures on the wall for everybody to see. On the positive side, incentives can be given for good performance and open productivity tracking used as a positive motivational tool.

Ultimately, it is important for the company that productivity increases, as that is the basis for cost decrease and profitability increase. To find this out, productivity is measured by KPIs that exhibit how many operations or activities an FTE can perform in a specified period of time. A productivity measurement could be the amount of invoices handled by one FTE per year, the amount of fixed-asset bookings made per year or the amount of orders received per year. In all assets, productivity will be measured by FTE, not persons, to make figures comparable.

Most of the productivity increases are reached by simply automating activities previously performed by a human. As an example, content of an incoming invoice was previously input into the ERP system by copying and keying in the figures by hand. Technology enables companies today to use a scanner and optical character recognition (OCR) software to copy automatically the content from a paper invoice to the ERP system. The employee in this process set-up only needs to verify the amounts by visually checking the screen. This verification activity takes less time than the keying in of figures. So to perform the invoice reception activities, it takes less time per invoice and thus more invoices per year can be handled. Productivity in the invoice reception process increases and the activity performed by the employee actually is (for most employees) more satisfying then the keying in of figures. From a benefit point of view, the cost of the technology necessary must be balanced against the productivity gains possible. Hence, in companies with larger volumes, technology pays for itself faster. This is a major benefit of the SSO, because it enables smaller companies or smaller entities to reach higher volumes by pooling the individual volumes.

Technology that the individual entities could not afford before now becomes affordable to the group. Productivity gains are reached by using processes and technologies many of which used to be referred to as 'e-business'. An SSO actually is the place where the e-business activities are concentrated. An SSO as such is based on utilizing some of the e-technology, mainly to automate and decrease human paper-handling necessity. Even though the new economy has been determined dead, e-business is actually still alive and with us more than ever and the processes in an SSO are a consequent implementation of e-thinking.

Service level improvements

Research equally proves, that service levels improve with the set-up of SSOs (see Table 23). The logic behind this is that in an SSO environment the SSO has to listen more to the demands of its customers than did the individual finance departments before in the old pre-SSO structure. The SSO is a service unit or business partner that has to satisfy customer needs. Hence it will engage in more communication with customers than was the case before. This communication will help both sides gain a better overview of the complete process and break down functional barriers. By understanding what the other side of the process looks like and what the needs and priorities of the partner are, the process can be improved and the satisfaction level of the customer increases.

Table 23   SSO's estimated impact on overall customer service

	% of centres	
	To date (%)	In 3 years (%)
Greater than 2% decrease	6	2
0% +/- 2% impact	28	5
3–10% increase	21	19
11–20% increase	35	44
Greater than 20% increase	10	30

A high customer satisfaction level is important for the SSO because of its role as a professional service organization. It has to prove that it is working – that it can deliver the same quality of service as the individual entities did before, or better. Failing to reach these service levels that satisfy the customer can threaten the pure existence of the SSO. If clients complain strongly about the service levels, the company leadership might be forced to dismantle the SSO and return to the state before the introduction of the SSO.

An added difficulty in delivering sufficient service levels and measuring them is that, in a pre-SSO environment, finance departments often did not measure customer satisfaction, because there was no 'customer'. Some companies do not want to ask the service receiver (even when starting an SSO) what they think about the service, so as 'not to rock the boat'. It is perceived that the 'customers' were happy with what they got before and 'it worked', so they should not be bothered with questions about customers' wishes. Otherwise they would come up with unrealistic expectations and make it even more difficult for the SSO to prove that it can perform its service tasks properly.

The short answer is: this road will lead to nowhere. The reason is simple: the benefits gained from open communication in terms of process understanding and optimization potential are greater by far than the quantity of 'unrealistic' new wishes from the customers. Sticking with the previous service content and level and little communication about it is a sign of being in a centralized environment, but not in an SSO. This could well be a workable solution but it will miss out on significant opportunities.

In SSOs, the customers do actually increase their expectation levels. The mere fact that measurements are now available makes them think about their expectations, and require improvements. Before, the measurements mostly did not exist, so the level of service was not measurable. Nevertheless, the open communication environment will help explain what can be done and the customers will be willing to accept good solutions. Also, by measuring the performance in the pre-SSO set-up, a baseline can be fixed to help the SSO prove the actual performance development. A service level agreement (SLA) will be a valuable tool also, from a change management point of view, to help facilitate this discussion between SSO and customer, because it requires both sides to discuss the service levels and their pricing and enables both sides to understand better the issues of the other side.

The services, their levels and the SLA all have to change over time to meet changing requirements. Hence the continuous measurement of service levels, a communication and control activity schedule between customer and SSO and the transfer of client requests into SSO-internal process improvement teams is elementary for the long-term success of an SSO. Unfortunately, the service levels are not deemed highly important by many companies thinking of SSO. That is a sign that cost reduction is their only major target. It is important to note that failing to fulfil certain service levels, normally at least the levels that existed prior to the SSO, will most probably lead to an unsuccessful end of either the project or the established SSO.

Process quality improvements

Process quality is not as easy to measure as some other benefits, such as cost benefits. This is due to the difficulty in agreeing what the quality measures are. It is often a question of what is perceived to be important by the different process players. The easiest measures are around failures in the process: measuring errors. It is possible to find error measurements in almost all processes – booking errors, payment errors and so on. Measurement can be a combination of errors in relation to time, for instance booking errors per FTE per year or invoices not handled inside a specific time frame. Depending on the definition of the time requirements, quality levels defined as a target equalling 100% can vary significantly. The measurements can target a number of complaints from other functions, customers or employees. Quality could also be defined overall as a degree of satisfaction of the customer, perhaps the results of a customer satisfaction survey. Quality can be linked to the service levels as the requirement to fulfil the defined service levels in as many cases as possible. Quality hence is more difficult to benchmark against that of other companies because of the different individual requirements. Nevertheless, quality is important as a factor in the total SSO performance scan and needs to be tracked. Fortunately for those who are thinking of an SSO, research proves a positive relationship between SSOs and process quality. It is naturally a view of companies comparing their previous and post-SSO situation.

Table 24   SSO's estimated impact on overall process quality

	% of centres	
	To date (%)	In 3 years (%)
Greater than 2% decrease	2	2
0% +/- 2% impact	21	2
3–10% increase	25	16
11–20% increase	36	43
Greater than 20% increase	16	37

Quality and cost improvements in SSOs mostly advance hand in hand. An optimized process will improve quality as well as productivity, resulting in customer satisfaction and cost benefits. Higher quality reduces the volume of errors and complaint-solving activities, hence increasing the relative amount of initially value-adding activities and reducing double-work. High-quality processes and process outputs are also a core requirement for reaching internally high employee satisfaction, as any employee is influenced negatively by bad quality and the resulting number of queries, complaints and frustration with which they must deal.

Compliance issues and risk reduction

At the time of writing, when we have experienced the accounting scandals of all the Enrons and Worldcoms, and when new legislation (such as Sarbanes-Oxley) has been imposed on companies regarding accounting, risk control and related fields, it would be wise to consider compliance and risk issues connected with finance operations and their move to an SSO. Most companies view an SSO project as risky and identify lots of risks in reducing local finance presence. In fact, any business action entails some level of risk and implementing an SSO is truly loaded with risks because of its nature as a complex organizational and process-change exercise with lots of change management issues related to it. We will look further at risk later in this chapter under 'Critical success factors', and in Part II, dealing with the implementation issues.

Apart from those implementation risks that are mainly related to achieving the defined goals inside the defined time-line and dealing with risks that are inherent risks to the SSO set-up itself, the question here is whether risk could be reduced and compliance increased by an SSO, and could hence be a benefit or drawback criterion.

As an example, a large consumer-goods company decided to go for an SSO based on a list of reasons, of which one was the reduction of risk and improvement of compliance with legal and regulatory requirements. The company had literally hundreds of entities scattered around the world, each with a finance department which, in most cases, was small. As a result the company was not able, despite its name and brands, to attract the level of finance talent it required. The prospect of working in a small finance department for a small company specialized not in finance but in consumer goods was not appealing to possible recruits. Even good salaries cannot compensate for everything. Over time, this led to a lot of internal audit reports exhibiting substantial problems in coping with the compliance issues of the group. The set-up of country and regional SSOs was perceived as a good method of pooling finance people to reduce compliance issues by more centralized control on policy adherence and increase the attractiveness of the finance function to potential candidates to be hired. The quality of people could be increased and compliance issues reduced. Hence, the SSO was a way to reduce the company's risk of being drawn into litigation and other legal fights and to reduce double-work connected with the low quality of finance work. Also, internal audit can benefit as audit activities can be reduced and audit time-lines increased.

An SSO clearly can be a beneficial set-up for both small and large companies in improving the ability to cope with compliance issues. This will increase quality and hence reduce external risk. It is difficult to put a price tag on the benefits of risk reduction, as they only show as avoided costs, but it is worth considering these benefits in an SSO appraisal. Lots of new requirements are and always will be imposed on companies regarding their accounting activities. Shareholders and other stakeholders have an interest in the validity of reported figures. As a result regulations such as Sarbanes-Oxley (SARBOX) are issued. The main effects of SARBOX on SSOs are:

- strict period closing deadlines

- detailed documentation requirements.

An SSO will normally have closing times far below the 30 days at the fiscal year end required by SARBOX (for companies listed by the Securities and Exchange Commission or SEC) and hence have no activity resulting from this. Companies with longer closing times need to shorten their closing process, to redesign their process to meet the deadline. One consumer-goods company spent half a million US dollars to perform this activity. This is not an unusual size of money to be spent on a Fast Close or Lean Close project. SSOs mostly have best-practice processes in place and rarely need 30 days to close. Companies such as Oracle with an SSO close in just two to four days. High-quality processes in an SSO will always be better equipped in meeting new requirements, especially when they have international reach.

Another example is that of two telecommunication companies. As a result of SARBOX process documentation requirements, one of the telecommunication companies (without SSO) spent two million US dollars in two months to document properly all the different processes across different countries. Another similar company stated that it had a standard process and complete documentation on these processes available in its SSO. No additional activity was necessary. An SSO will enable companies to meet new legal and regulatory requirements better. The next win for companies with SSO will be meeting the International Financial Reporting Standards (IFRS) requirements when imposed on Europe.

BENEFITS FOR PEOPLE AND CULTURE

Some companies struggle with the fact that they think they are 'not ready' for SSO. The background of this is a company culture assessment. It can be very difficult to change the company culture. Other companies feel that a cultural change is not required as they feel they have the right culture.

Whatever the case, an SSO is a chance to set up an operation wherein the organization's culture can be redefined or improved. Especially in a greenfield approach, setting up an SSO 'from scratch' will enable the architects also to design a culture that fits the operational purpose of the SSO. Companies that struggle to change anything because of, for example, a very decentralized structure and 'democratic' decision-making culture, might want to consider an SSO as a new platform that can be utilized to move activities over time into a new environment. This way can be easier than trying to convince all the 'old players' to change their views and working ways. Hence, an SSO offers a platform and opportunity to change company culture inside finance and accounting departments more easily than without an SSO and to reach targets otherwise not reachable.

A German nutritional company some years ago set up an SSO in the same city as its HQ, not far from that specific site. Still, it was difficult to convince the old employees to move to the new location and new environment that were set up as a separate service company with a unique service culture. The changes took place nevertheless. Years later an organizational split of the company led to the assessment of a possible reintegration of some of these activities performed in the SSO. Interestingly, the biggest resistance came from those same employees. Their reasoning was: 'In the old company we were considered to be back-office and of lower importance and hence treated like the fifth wheel on a car. In the SSO we are accepted to be providing a professional service worth something.'

Even though people in general fear change and are mostly reluctant to support and accept it, an SSO can improve job satisfaction levels and serve as the motivation to improve even individual performances. Also, because an SSO has more specific job roles, employees might lose some variety in their jobs. On the other hand they have higher expertise levels in their jobs and through job rotation and other supporting measures can over time satisfy their learning goals and advance within the total organization. SSOs can be very good jumping boards for advancing into high corporate roles. This has happened in many companies that implemented an SSO. Project leaders and SSO directors tend to be sought-after people when important positions are being staffed.

BENEFITS FROM SSO COMPARED TO FRAGMENTED EFFORTS

Many companies review the SSO concept, and then respond that it will not be applicable to them, because they have already performed all the activities contained in it. They state that process re-engineering has been done many times, the organization has been redesigned and they also have a new IT system in place. Hence, they conclude, SSO cannot deliver anything on top of that. Research over 12 years shows that SSOs can and will open up an additional 30% optimization opportunity for these companies. This is due to the fact that fragmented efforts miss about 30% of the potentials (on average) because the integration of the IT components, process and organization is not tackled. These are exactly the main components of an SSO concept.

The hard work in an SSO implementation is in 'putting together the puzzle', that is, linking processes with IT and organization. This exercise, as painful as it might sometimes be, will tap into that integration potential not touched by individual projects.

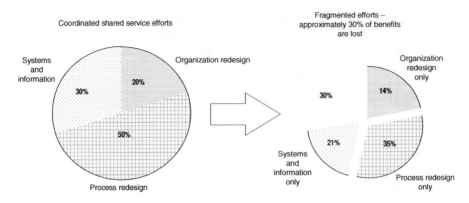

Figure 11   Historical comparison between results from fragmented efforts versus single effort (SSO)

CRITICAL SUCCESS FACTORS

Any project has critical success factors (CSFs). An SSO project has them too and they are useful to consider as they will help decide whether the project has been set up correctly and what to consider to be successful. They have direct impact on reaching the goals and hence delivering the benefits sought.

The five most important factors for success in implementation are:

1.   Top management support (84%).

2.   Emphasizing a mentality of 'change management' during the entire project (64%).

3.   Recruiting appropriate employees for the SSC (59%).

4.   Communicating the project goals to employees early and efficiently (47%).

5.   Quick wins in order to build momentum (31%).

The one main critical success factor is top-management support. It is actually surprising that 'only' 84% of companies mentioned this and not the expected 100% (historically comparable figures going back to 1999 are between 84% and 87%). Our research on over 700 companies with an SSO shows that merely one of them stated having been successful in implementing SSO 'bottom-up' without support from top management. In this case the project was taken to a very far stage without a budget and dedicated resources and then management was confronted with the facts. Finally approval of course was given, but it does not seem to be the advisable way to proceed.

Top-management support needs to be more than just the statement in a board room that it should be done. It needs to be visible top-management support, so to ease the way for the implementation teams and to convince opponents as early as possible that the SSO decision is strongly supported from the top and will be carried out. Hence, top management has to participate in a range of meetings and renew the supporting statements publicly. In some cases this is hard to achieve for the project team, as top management often wants to keep a back door open. It is important for the project team to take the project past a 'no-return' point quickly and convince management by presenting so-called 'quick wins' to help decision-making in favour of SSO.

The other CSFs are around people issues: having the right people in the project and in the SSO, dealing with change management issues and performing substantial communication efforts. One international manufacturing company stated in its management presentation to the CFO that the relevance and required relative amount of workload in the change management area was up to 50% of the SSO project. Unfortunately many companies concentrate on technology and process issues and do not want to invest in the change management topic. Some companies state that the changes will be 'ordered' and employees will have to 'just do it'. Experience shows that this approach will not work as well as the communicative open approach.

It is worth stating that possible factors, such as choosing the right technology or defining a specific organizational set-up, do not appear on the list.

RISKS OF SETTING UP AN SSO

The risks of setting up an SSO are the flip side of the experience of companies that have done it, comprising the things that 'went wrong'. Again, people-based issues constitute most of the threats.

The highest risks when setting up an SSO are:

1. Poor service quality (52%).

2. IT problems (47%).

3. Little employee support (40%).

4. Business activities are interrupted during implementation (31%).

5. High implementation costs (21%).

6. Other (17%).

Poor service quality is in many research reports stated as the number-one risk. We make reference to the comments on service quality above. It is surely very difficult to be successful if the customers of the service centre do not support the SSO. An added difficulty in terms of making the customers happy is that their expectations always increase dramatically when an SSO is implemented. The SSO provides more transparency on services, their quality levels and costs, and enables customers for the first time actually to rate the service they are getting, so managing expectations is critical in order to influence the customers' perceived satisfaction rating.

IT problems occur quite frequently during an SSO implementation, which is not a surprise since many SSO implementations are connected with an ERP implementation or process redesign including functionality changes in systems. In most cases the reasons for this are lack of resources, bad preparation, unrealistic time-lines and going live without testing and back-up. There are lots of horror stories told about ERP implementations. One IT company introduced a new materials management (MM) module in service advertising protocol (SAP), resulting in a situation where no goods whatsoever could be delivered. The sales force then drove around and visited clients with a load of products in their car trunks and delivered whatever they needed. A chain reaction could be prevented in most cases but the cost of this activity was significant.

Business activities are sometimes endangered when things go badly wrong. A logistics company was unable to send out invoices for almost six months resulting in serious liquidity problems. The parent company had to inject cash to secure the going concern. In many cases, there will be a backlog of invoices to be paid when the transfer to the SSC takes place. Often this is not known or the quantity of open incoming invoices had not been made transparent by the local accounting departments. This results in extra work that can only be solved by additional resources. The transfer itself can also create a backlog, as new employees are slower in the beginning and productivity decreases. It is important to provide for transfer-related resource peaks to be able to reduce the backlog fast.

An automotive supplier had about 15 000 unpaid invoices and had to have one resource count them manually every week to monitor the performance, thereby further reducing the personnel available to actually work on the invoices. An automotive company fell into a payment backlog of three or four months, resulting in angry vendors calling the AP clerks and threatening them personally since their companies were having serious financial difficulties due to the cash not coming in.

There are further 'horror stories' and, as real as they are, it is important to remember that these risks can be mitigated by properly following all the necessary steps in an SSO implementation. In any SSO implementation companies will experience the so-called 'hockey-stick effect' (see Figure 12). The effect is similar to what happens in any other implementation project (such as ERP) or change initiative. After the go-live or cut-over date, resources and costs will increase for a transition period. At the same time performance and quality will be reduced. The risks mentioned above can materialize if no counter-activities are performed.

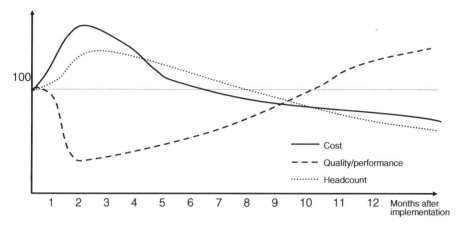

Figure 12   'The 'hockey-stick effect'

Mitigation measures include preparing for the hockey-stick effect, in other words hoarding some excess resources for this limited time period – either keeping some of the local resources that will be outplaced for some months longer or building up excess capacity in the SSC. These can be people who are kept for further use in other process areas or will become necessary due to anticipated volume increases in future. Another measure is to have a very good performance measurement system in place that includes baseline data from before the cut-over as well as from monitoring KPIs in the transition period. The discussion of these KPIs will enable all participants to reduce their emotional excitement about 'things having been better before' and 'nothing working properly in the SSC', focus on the factual data and concentrate on moving the organization into the right direction. The hockey-stick effect can lead to performance drops of up to 50% or more, although it normally does not occur in all process areas at the same time and in the same strength. Overall, a 20–30% drop for some two to four months has to be expected and managed. The performance drop should be covered in the SLAs so no contractual discussions arise based on short-term implementation issues.

Equally, other functions have to support the SSO. Processes often run through the SSO, but have links to other functions, such as warehousing, procurement and sales. If they do not carry out their part of the process, success is endangered. In purchase-to-pay (PTP), for example, if invoices without purchase orders (POs) are sent for verification to individual purchasers or departments and they do not deliver back their approval or missing data, the SSO is not able to match its timely deadlines for performance in booking and paying the invoices. Although the process can be optimized by workflow to help drive the invoice verification, there are thousands of process links that could be used by other functions to 'work against the SSO'.

It is helpful to implement the CSFs mentioned above to solve these issues and mitigate the risks.

REASONS NOT TO SET UP AN SSO

Not everybody actually does set up an SSO, even if a complete feasibility study has been performed, maybe even with positive financial outcomes. Reasons to decide against an SSO are mostly based on two criteria:

- there is no 'burning platform'
- an SSO is perceived as being a strategic misfit.

The 'burning platform' is mostly characterized by the need to save costs. Companies with extremely strong financial results do not feel the pressure to change things. An agribusiness company told us that their gross margin was 50% and the perceived saving in finance of 1–2% of revenue was not appealing enough to them. We congratulated them on the excellent market positioning they had and wished them well. It is difficult to make a case, even if it financially makes sense, when the urgency is not there. An automotive company stated that the calculated run rate savings of 10–15 million euros were not high enough in absolute terms to make them seriously think about 'setting a fire' or 'going through the difficulties of trying to change the organization'. Other companies would be excited about 1 to 2% improvements in their bottom line of 10 million in savings but, as in everything, this is always relative.

Some companies accept that there are benefits to be gained, but fear the negative effects on other parts of the organization or on their overall culture. These are corporations with independent business units or strong country organizations completely responsible for the business. The 'rules of the game', they feel, are not allowing them to give centralized guidance on how to administer the businesses. Therefore, they state that an SSO does not fit their strategy.

Other reasons not to set up an SSO include:

- it does not fit the strategy of the company (55%)
- there is a lack of critical mass/volumes (27%)
- other (18%).

Actually, the areas in the scope of the SSO by definition are support functions and hence are not strategic. Therefore, setting up an SSO should not be a strategic issue. Nevertheless, the set-up of those companies in reality does not enable them to 'take away' the responsibility of running these local or individual administrations. At least it is a major change effort and puts the bar quite high.

Lack of critical mass is another reason why some companies opt not to go for an SSO. Sometimes the perceived lack of volumes is incorrect. The principle of SSOs also supports smaller volumes and centres with under 20 FTEs are not uncommon. Small finance departments can actually be a good reason to look at SSCs as a way to create more mass and solve issues such as lack of talent, inefficiencies and compliance issues.

Other reasons, such as language problems and legal and regulatory fears, have been widely eliminated, partly by improvements in the framework conditions (such as more flexible legal frameworks in EU or Asian countries such as China), partly by education proving some fears are unnecessary, for instance language issues.

Fears remaining, even in companies that might have done some feasibility work, include uncertainty about the actual return on investment (ROI) and the change readiness of their organization. These fears can be mitigated by detailed preparation work. The readiness issue is one where it is best to evaluate realistically external comparisons to discover what the status quo really looks like. If the company is not ready, SSO might still remain a reasonable goal; it is just that the path to get there is longer and will include more change management upfront.

Information deficits and fears in relation to an SSO include:

1. 'We do not have enough information to quantify the ROI' (19%).

2. 'We do not know if our processes are ready for an SSO' (12%).

3. 'We do not know if our organization is able to take this change' (8%).

4. 'We do not know if our IT can support shared services' (4%).

IT fears are not uncommon, but can be all solved. They are mostly not of a technical type but based on fears about large investments and acceptance inside the organization. This situation also can be tackled by stable preparation steps.

On the positive side, it is worth noting that 77% of European companies in 2003 have performed a feasibility study and feel that they have sufficient information about all relevant aspects of implementing an SSO. This is up significantly from the 2002 figures and suggests a much better preparation phase in most companies than in previous years. Also, more mature case examples are available to learn from and the starting position gets easier year by year.

COMMISSIONAIRE STRUCTURE AND TAX-RELATED BENEFITS AND RISKS

Tax is relevant to every company and any project on the type of SSO will have to deal with tax issues. In an SSO project there are a load of tax issues, especially when it has an international scope. There can be tax effects also, but in terms of benefits and risks it is important to note that the set-up of an SSO as such is tax-neutral.

Setting up an SSO is not an organizational change triggered by tax-saving potentials. However, an SSO is often discussed in connection with other organizational changes such as setting up a commissionaire model (also called '3P' or 'trading company structure'). The commissionaire model works based on a simple logic: risk brings reward – the greater the risk, the higher the reward will be. Based on this, companies try to move risk by moving activities and personnel to a lower-cost country. The risk sitting in this lower-tax environment can be taxed there and the overall tax burden is thereby reduced. Because it is necessary to move some quantity of activities and people physically to this country of the so-called principal company, it is possible and even probable that the location decision for an SSO and the process flows inside the company will be affected by a commissionaire model set-up.

Philosophically, the commissionaire model and SSO fit together just fine, because both are based on centralized provision or control of activities, strict guidelines and documented standardized process flows. The project of setting up an SSO in parallel with a commissionaire model will have a different twist to it, as the tax-savings target is often the overriding goal and synergies and other efficiencies are seen as a nice-to-have side product. This is also true for similar models involving stripped-risk entities, buy-sell models and toll manufacturing.

If a trading company is in existence when the SSO project runs, it is possible that this will affect the scope of the project. A country or business unit with a trading company structure might lose significant tax advantages if the structure is changed. It might be, therefore, that the finance and accounting activities are not toughened, so as not to endanger the tax model acceptance by local tax authorities, resulting in that country being left out of the SSO. The main tax benefits possible of an SSO project are connected to the location selection, because some countries offer special SSO tax treatment. This can be connected with beneficial tax treatment of SSO executives.

CHAPTER 4

IT for Shared Service Organizations

THE IMPORTANCE OF IT

It is important to make the statement again and again: 'IT is the enabler for shared services'. An SSO project and an SSO operation without IT support is unthinkable. Or, in other words: shared services would not be possible without the opportunity provided by today's IT platforms and IT tools.

As stated before, an SSO is, among other things, based on the fact that geographical distance does not matter because it can be overcome. The tool to overcome it is IT. Most employees have experienced the benefits of company networks enabling them to, for example, print a document out on different printers located in different offices across the building. Naturally this also works in other buildings than their own and even over large distances as proximity does not matter from an IT point of view. Equally, data can be transferred and received over large distances by IT: over e-mail, the intranet, the Internet, and so on. Remote access, the ability to access applications from other locations, is no longer an obstacle from an IT point of view. Hence, IT enables organizations to connect people and workplaces with each other, even if they are physically apart. Telecommunications take care of the verbal connection and are today based on IT too.

The success of an SSO is largely dependent on a strong IT platform. Depending on the individual company, the IT is in place before an SSO is built, or IT needs to be upgraded to match the SSO's requirements. In any case, cooperation with IT and consideration of the company's current and future IT landscape is of great importance.

THE IT LANDSCAPE

An integrated ERP is still the major enabler and ERP in general is viewed as the most useful IT solution (68%) to support the SSO approach. It is actually quite surprising that the remainder of companies do not think an ERP system is critical for the success of an SSO. Maybe this is because the importance of an ERP backbone is viewed as self-explanatory and hence is not mentioned specifically.

The anticipated most useful technology solutions include:

1. ERP (68%).

2. Workflow (46%).

3. Data warehouse (46%).

4. Data analysis and reporting tools (28%).

5. Intranet (26%).

6. Imaging (24%).

7. Automatic matching and payment allocation tools (23%).

8. e-procurement (23%).

9. Self-service capabilities (19%).

10. EDI (19%).

11. CRM (8%).

12. Activity-based costing (ABC) tools (8%).

13. Call-centre tools (7%).

14. XML (7%).

However, the set-up of uniform and integrated systems has only been achieved by 35% of the companies. Due to historically very autonomous IT decision-making (often by division, business unit, legal entity or inside the geographic cluster), 65% of companies operate on the basis of heterogeneous IT landscapes. In these cases companies do try for multisystem SSOs, which of course also work, but even in those cases several ERPs are the backbone of success.

Workflow (46%) and data warehouses (46%) have become preferred and almost standard solutions. An automotive company told us that amongst the three most important learnings from a five-year-old SSC implementation was the fact that 'you should never implement a PTP process without workflow'. A range of other IT solution tools is increasing in importance. Best-practice processes without a selection of additional IT tools, especially workflow and data warehouse, would be unthinkable today, even though only about 50% of companies actually use workflow.

In Europe, SAP retains and improves its leading position as the most widely used ERP platform (76%) validating last year's anticipated trend (71%). Oracle has increased in utilization in Europe from 7% in 2002 to 14% in 2003 and PeopleSoft has now been mentioned by 4% as their backbone system. The spread in individual countries differs significantly. In UK as well as outside Europe (the US, South Africa, and so on) packages from Oracle have a much stronger market positioning than in continental Europe.

Table 25   Utilization of ERP systems

	2002 (%)	Today (%)
SAP	71	76
Oracle	7	14
Peoplesoft	0	4
Baan	2	3
Other standard software	25	25
Custom-built software	11	10

In terms of the SSO, it does not matter which ERP system you use or choose, as long as it is an integrated package covering the end-to-end processes and allowing the processes to run via an SSO. Most packages support SSOs or at least do not rule them out.

BENEFITS BROUGHT BY IT

It is actually remarkable that, despite suboptimal systems, European-based companies have still been able to achieve significant savings. This validates Hackett's finding that European companies, as a baseline, in general perform some 20% less efficiently than the worldwide average. Significant potential for improvement therefore did exist and still exists in the consolidation of resources and implementation of best practices in organization and process. Also, significant potentials remain in IT standardization and consolidation. Companies with integrated, standardized and consolidated IT platforms are over 40% more efficient than companies in non-standardized environments (see Table 26).

Table 26   Effect of system complexity on finance cost (as a percentage of revenue)

	2002 total cost of finance (%)	2002 transaction processing cost (%)
Many systems, non-standardized, decentralized	1.44	0.50
Few systems, standardized, centralized	0.80	0.29
Difference	*-44%*	*-42%*

That said, there are still significant additional optimization opportunities for all companies. It is very clear, though, that IT is the enabler for SSO and a standardized ERP platform is the enabler for the world-class performance of the SSO.

The effect of aggressive rationalization of systems complexity can be proven empirically to be driving significantly lower finance costs for world-class companies. The curve becomes extremely steep only when the difference is between one and two systems or two and three systems. It is interesting to see that the real differences in finance cost are not dependent on whether a company has five, ten or 50 systems – here the curve is quite flat. So in terms of system reduction, the benefits kick in when the reduction is from three to two systems and two to one system. Another view to prove the point is that in the database of Hackett, out of those companies that overall rank as world-class, 100% operate on one ERP system. Amongst average companies the figure is 79%.

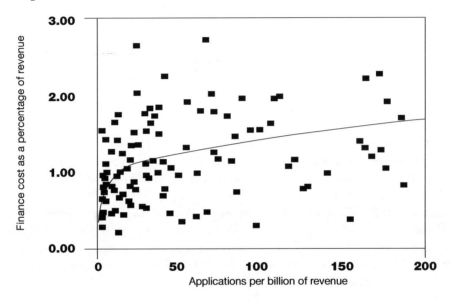

Figure 13   Effect of system complexity (number of systems) on finance cost

Companies often assume that those competitors who claim to operate only one global ERP have reached this by setting up a significant amount of subsystems, such as additional databases, special billing systems and reporting and planning tools on top of their ERP. Actually, world-class companies also have fewer subsystems than average companies. The feeder ratio, measuring the amount of additional secondary systems in relation to each primary application (ERP) stands at 1.3 for world-class companies and 3.5 for average companies. Hence, world-class companies in general operate on fewer systems than average companies. It is also worth remembering that IT alone will not deliver world-class results. As discussed above, the full benefits always depend on actively improving IT, processes and organization.

SELF-SERVICE APPLICATIONS

Self-service applications are sometimes regarded as being a type of shared service, sometimes not. Actually, self-service is exactly the opposite of shared services, as the service is not provided centrally but instead moved to the user/customer and performed individually by the user/customer. However, self-service is an important component of any SSO, as it has a significant effect on the scope and the central–local split of processes. Activities performed through self-service do not need to be performed by the SSO. Also, self-service has to be enabled by standard policies, processes and a high-performance IT platform. Most self-service processes run on a Web basis. Hence, self-service processes are mainly contingent on a well-defined process based on strong IT support.

Self-services are mostly used in HR processes. To start with, employees could perform name and address changes and changes of other master data such as bank accounts, by Web instead of filling out forms that are then sent to HR for someone to key in into possibly even several systems. Inputting data directly by the employee saves on cost and also reduces error probability significantly. The employees are the ones who know their address and bank account number best, so little checking, apart from standard mismatch checks and the like, are necessary. The access can be restricted or shared by authority concepts with different entry levels.

In certain HR processes, savings from self-service are significant. In the health and welfare process, first-quartile companies with self-service are 70% more cost efficient than first-quartile companies without self-service. A number of companies has set up intranets with access to benefits accounts, overviews of pension plans, status of T&E and so on.

For finance, self-services are an excellent addition to best-practice process design based on the centralized provision of services. Process links to HR can often be covered by self-service, as can parts of payroll and T&E (if in scope). The other possible direction of providing self-services is to enable customers or vendors to access the company systems from outside for a limited view on, say, delivery status, payables and receivables status or open items. Vendors and customers can be enabled to input master data changes over the Internet – billing data changes, order numbers, address changes, VAT numbers and so on. Naturally, this kind of data will have to run through an internal validation before being transferred into the master-data database. Changes to bank accounts of the receiver in particular should be validated before significant payments are made to that new account.

IT plays a key role in this area. All the nice ideas possible can only be realized if the IT landscape allows it. Hence, an SSO set-up should include the consideration of self-services and the necessary IT tools to run them.

THE E-BUSINESS PLATFORM AND E-SSC

An SSO is the centre of all e-business activities. Most people don't think about the SSO in that way, but actually all relevant processes using e-technology run through the SSO. Almost all e-business activities are included in OTC and PTP, which are the most common process cycles in SSOs. An SSO needs to consider actual and planned e-activities of the company and link them with the SSO set-up and the self-service applications that are in place or planned. Again, IT is the platform on which all of these ideas will be realized. The selection of the right platform therefore is more than a selection of an ERP; it also includes the selection of necessary tools for workflow, Web access, database management and so on.

In the aftermath of the new economy, shared services were considered by some to be a rather conservative idea and talk was about e-shared services or e-SSCs. This is actually exactly what an SSO produces in any case. A good SSO always uses IT tools and new technologies to improve its processes. Those tools often are e-tools and an e-SSC actually is just an SSC that uses a significant number of IT tools and has largely automated processes with open process links to the outside world.

THE PROCESS LINK TO IT

The implementation of processes that fit with an SSO structure is dependent on the fit of the process design with the IT. There are several ways of designing processes and carrying out IT projects. Experience shows that best-practice solutions can differ but always have one thing in common: process design has to be an input to the IT implementation. If there is no detailed process design available as an input for IT, then IT will just carry over the functionalities from the previous systems to the new ERP.

Many companies have ERP implementation methodologies in place whereby the IT department will initially ask all functions to provide a list of system functionalities they require. These lists are treated as 'wish lists' and not all functionalities can be provided. Even though this is understandable, the problem is that prioritization of necessary functionalities and consideration of redesign effects are both missing. Certain functionalities available in the previous system set-up, such as cheque payments, might not be necessary in the future. However, self-billing might be the process to be used in the future and the systems might not provide for that. The company might decide to change from a three-way match to a two-way match or vice versa. This is, however, largely dependent on the system set-up.

Process design, hence, always needs to be an input for IT implementation. In terms of project set-up, it is advisable to work in mixed teams (finance plus IT). This is not the same as *communicating* between different teams. In reality there is a gap between the thinking and language of the IT and finance and one of the two sides has to bridge this gap. Practically it can only be finance. The finance people need to provide the process design on such a detailed level that IT can use it as an implementation guideline. This blueprint must detail the processes but also explain what functionalities (in IT language) are necessary.

'PLAIN VANILLA' ERP VERSUS STANDARD ERP

In terms of setting up a system, several companies discuss staying as close as possible to standard SAP or standard Oracle. This, in general, is a good idea. However, in some cases the desired ERP target is described as a 'plain vanilla' ERP. Now, it does not matter what you want to call it but, realistically, a plain vanilla system does not exist. In any ERP system, lots of switches have to be set: the system needs customizing. Customizing is not the same as programming new functionalities (using ABAP programming in SAP and so on). Customizing is a selection process where the system settings are chosen to match the desired process design. This selection is based on alternative settings provided by the 'standard' ERP. Examples (based on SAP) of choices you will have to make without changing the standard but substantially influencing the set-up are:

- valuated or non-valuated goods entry: results in differences in time of coding;

- cross-company postings allowed or not allowed: results in differences in intercompany reconciliation;

- business areas or profit centres: results in differences in working capital reporting;

- activating of fixed assets through direct posting or through SAP's IM/PS modules: results in differences in purchasing process and invoice verification.

It is critical that the necessity of process design as an input for IT customization is understood. The settings not only reflect the process design but often also the organizational roles. This holds true regardless of the order in which activities are performed. It is, however, easier to perform process design before IT customization, as the risk of not being able to implement best-practice processes is reduced to a minimum.

THE AUTONOMY TRAP

Many IT landscapes are characterized by the history of autonomous decision-making of single entities, business units or geographical clusters in terms of necessary systems. It is clear that different businesses have different requirements, but in some cases companies have given the decentralized decision-makers so much decision power that the system landscape has grown apart and become a jungle. It is surprising how some companies are able to operate successfully with, in some cases, hundreds of systems.

In the long run, the result of autonomous IT policy can be that the company is trapped in what we call the 'autonomy trap' (see Figure 14), which is the result of all business units and geographies having been autonomous in their IT decisions, resulting in a patchwork of systems.

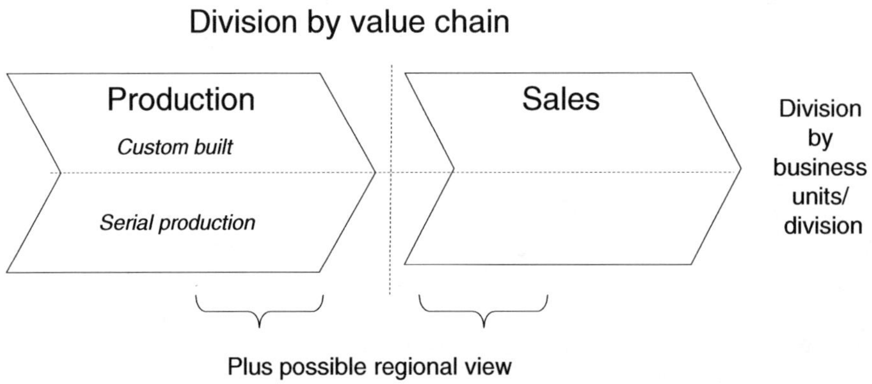

Division by value chain

Figure 14   The 'autonomy trap'

A large automotive company told us that they had not upgraded their SAP system for some years, as they feared the whole system would collapse if touched. An industrial-machinery producer told us that all businesses within the company could choose their own systems along the value chain, so production would have production systems, sales would have sales systems. These would then again be different in, say, serial production and custom-build production. Additionally, there is a geographical dimension, so a French serial production sales system could be different to the German serial production sales system.

One hopes these companies have provided for sufficient accruals for the day the system actually does need some fixing. Other companies can only be advised to try to not land in the autonomy trap and to get an IT framework strategy in place before it becomes too difficult to act.

THE INVOLVEMENT OF IT IN FINANCE SSOs

The role IT plays in a company internally is a major consideration for SSOs. In many cases IT is either a clear strategic role with a chief information officer (CIO) at its top setting a framework or a pure service provider trying hard to fulfil all the wishes the businesses have. On the one hand, IT should have a CIO at its top, so IT will be in a position to discuss successfully setting some borders to the freedoms inside system landscape. In past years, the amount of companies with a CIO role has increased from 65% (in 2000) to 82% (in 2002). Best-practice companies clearly find a healthy balance between the two extremes and have a CIO defining the IT strategy together with other top management. On the other hand, IT also has to provide services to the businesses. IT is a service unit, but the services should only be possible inside the defined strategic IT framework, for instance only using one strategic ERP platform. Having this balance in place will be supportive for an SSO project.

Additionally, it is useful to note that usage of IT is increasing steadily. In 2002, 84% of employees were qualified as IT end-users compared to 58% in 1999. Interestingly, the IT cost per end-user is not decreasing but increased from US$ 9.167 to US$ 11.656 per end-user. One would have expected some volume effects or synergies, but IT has obviously not delivered the ROI that was expected. The IT ROI is a different story, but for our purposes it is good to know that IT usage and IT costs are still rising. This means that large chunks of allocated costs of both the businesses (customers) and the SSO will be produced by the IT services used. Hence, the finance SSO should actively try to integrate IT people into the SSO project to be able, at least indirectly through process design and so on, to influence the IT cost that will be charged to them. IT should get involved also, to use what may be the only chance of moving to a single ERP platform and of cementing an IT strategy that will bear large cost and performance benefits to all sides.

Another discussion point is the differentiation and calculation of a finance SSO and IT business case and their linkage. We will discuss this in Part II.

IT SSO AND ITS CONNECTION WITH FINANCE SSO

Several companies have set up shared services in IT even before considering doing the same for finance and accounting (F&A). Due to the high complexity of the IT topic, a number of companies has gone directly to outsourcing IT systems, maintenance and operations or parts of those. Even if there has been a recent trend to re-insource some parts of IT, that does not seem to change the overall trend. It is rather a correction of contracting results and scoping errors of the original deal, and in some cases the normal customer reaction to unsatisfying service from a service provider.

So several companies will be in the situation that IT people have great understanding for a finance SSO project and the issues and difficulties associated with it, as they themselves have already gone through a similar experience, either for an IT

SSO or for IT outsourcing. This situation is beneficial for finance in its quest for SSO. IT should be considered an additional driver in this case. Even if IT is not organized as shared services, it certainly makes sense to become an SSO:

- In companies with an SSO, average operational support cost per end-user was US$ 3.082 (in 2002) and 24% lower than in companies without shared services.

- In companies with an SSO, the number of help-desk calls per end-user in a first-quartile company was 8.1 calls (in 2002) compared to 10.3 calls in a first-quartile company without shared services.

IT shared services is a best-practice concept to support the infrastructure, promote stronger communication, and cultivate centres of excellence for application development and support, including the help desk. Greater centralized control of IT operations delivers significant savings in operational support while simultaneously increasing performance.

The finance SSO implementation might also be a chance for IT to renew its structures. In this situation, however, not all players in IT will be necessarily happy about the finance SSO project due to their fears of the SSO idea being leveraged onto their jobs. It is necessary therefore to proceed with care and link up with the right persons to secure IT support.

CHAPTER 5

People – Incentives, Retention and Training

Any organization is mostly dependent on the people that work in it and for it. In an SSO this is as true as elsewhere. Even if processes are automated and there may be fewer people than before, the performance of the SSO is still impacted mostly by the personnel actually doing the job.

The most surprising thing about all those SSO projects of the last ten years is that even though basically everybody will agree that the people aspect is important, possibly the most important one, little funding is actually available for the people aspect of an SSO project. A project is often calculated based on technical skills necessary, technology that needs to be bought and organizational change costs. The only people issue always present in the business cases is the inclusion of severance costs as a major cost component. Expenditure on items such as training is often regarded debatable and as something 'nice to have'. There is a common belief that training does not 'pay off'. Even worse, a range of companies believes that change management consists mainly of 'ordering and demanding changes'. If a project content overview includes spending on items that are called change management, those activities are often taken off the list, as they are considered the management's core business and hence their internal responsibility.

It is worth spending some time on the topic that all think is the most important, but most spend no money on: people.

PEOPLE IN A TYPICAL SHARED SERVICE ORGANIZATION

A typical SSC is assumed to be something very different by those who have one and those who don't. Those companies not operating an SSC often fear it to be a large service production unit with thousands of data-input clerks, a kind of low-cost inputting factory. Others believe SSCs are only for large companies and cannot operate with small groups of people. In reality, the SSO concept is very flexible.

In Europe, 77% of SSCs have between 26 and 250 employees. Only 2% have over 500 employees but 12% are smaller than 25 employees. On a global basis the figures are similar, with the exception of large SSCs with over 500 employees, which had been set up by 14–15% (akris 2000–2001) of companies. So some of these 'transaction factories'

Table 27   Number of employees in established SSCs

Number of employees	%
1–10	6
11–25	6
26–50	15
51–100	34
101–250	28
251–500	10
501–1000	1
>1000	1

do exist, for example in India, but the large majority of SSCs are medium-sized groups of people.

A media company told us that when they reached about 200 employees in their SSC in Dublin, they set up a second centre. It seemed to be a manageable size and there were few additional benefits in growing the one centre compared to operating another SSC within one SSO. There does not exist an 'optimal size' of an SSC, but several companies seem to stop between 100 and 300 employees, as the SSC would otherwise need a service centre of its own.

Looking at the structure of people employed – or the people mix – the profile of world-class finance organizations is distinctly different from that of the average: 25% fewer managers (26% of total), 31% more professionals (59% of total), 51% broader span of control at 14.0 persons and fewer professional resources allocated to routine transaction processes (47% in world-class compared to 55% in average companies).

Now this is exactly the result of an SSO. In SSOs the span of control can be significantly higher than in traditional organizations that typically manage between five and ten employees per supervisor. In SSOs the ratio can easily be 15 or 20 and has in some organizations reached 40–50. Because SSOs have a higher degree of standardization, there are fewer operational issues on a daily basis that need to be solved and one supervisor can manage his or her time better.

The effect of an SSO on the people mix is logical, because through automation several of the more simple work steps can be reduced. Hence, fewer clerical people, relative to others, are necessary. Also, the higher span of control leads to excess capacities on the middle management level, hence resulting in fewer managers relative to others. This does not mean that the absolute figure of professionals will necessarily increase, as the total number of FTEs required is lower. This effect is seen in all best-practice organizations. In HR SSO, for example, the result is similar (see Table 28). The same effect on the staff mix will take place in any SSO and the administrative activities are the ones that are reduced in a world-class organization.

Table 28   Staffing comparison of world-class HR organizations versus average companies

Staff allocation by group	Average (%)	World-class (%)
Administration	56	26
Employee life-cycle	36	58
Decision support	6	14
Function management	2	3
Staff allocation by level		
Manager	29	19
Professional	35	58
Clerical	36	23

In summary, the people characteristics of a first-quartile shared service organization prove that organizational capability is driven by effective team-based structures. SSOs have fewer management layers and hence a flat hierarchy. Ninety-one per cent of European SSOs reported having a flat hierarchy organized in teams.

People characteristics of a first-quartile SSO include:

- Span of control is broader, at 10.3 as opposed to 7.2 for average.

- There are fewer layers of management and more direct involvement (fewer than two layers within the centre).

- Investment in training provides for more than six days of training per year per employee (mixture of soft and hard skills).

- Flatter organization enables fewer job grades and reduces complexity (four job grades against 8.3 for average).

- Results are reflected in lower turnover rates of 5.3%.

INCENTIVES, CAREER PATHS AND RETENTION

The fear of many employees in the 'old' F&A organizations is that an SSO will be a somewhat separate unit with few connections to the remaining organization and few career perspectives for themselves. In some cases they are right. It is, however, up to the individual company to define the role of its SSO and the links to the remaining organization. Several companies have proven that both the SSO project and operative work in the SSO can be excellent jumping boards for a career inside the corporation. It is therefore necessary to define career opportunities inside and outside the SSO and communicate them to all affected employees early enough.

Often employees are reluctant to provide a substantial part of their time for project work because they prefer to keep their operative work on track. This is understandable, as they often do not know how sure it is that the SSO will become active and how secure it would be as a workplace. The company's management needs to communicate clearly the decision on the implementation of an SSO and respective line managers need to discuss with their employees the possibilities inside the SSO and within the whole group. Only if management succeeds in convincing the employees of the perspectives in an SSO, will they put substantial efforts into the project work and be willing to transfer to an SSO.

It is useful to have a detailed communication plan in place and differentiate between different groups of employees, dividing them into three categories:

- those who will be kept
- those who are necessary for the time of the project
- those who can be outplaced.

Management has just one chance to do the right things about communication. Once rumours start going around, it is difficult to correct them. A proactive stand on communication is essential. The benefits that can be offered to employees can vary, but certainly include:

- training
- job rotation inside the SSO
- definition of the SSO as basic training and laying out what specific jobs are available after that (perhaps in local accounting, in controlling, in project management and so on)
- performance bonuses (individual and team-based).

SSOs in general have higher fluctuation. Most companies would initially view that as negative. However, some companies have stated that they have a fluctuation rate of 20%, but would rather have 25%. Others feel that 5% is already a problem. This view will depend for one thing on the company culture and whether the 'old' culture has been taken over to the SSO. If it has been, then the SSO is often measured by the previous standards. This might not be useful, because a well-managed SSO will have efficient processes in place and also have a defined training schedule. A best-practice SSO can train people in days or weeks instead of months and can therefore cope better with fluctuation. Fluctuation can be a benefit, as salary levels can be kept at a lower level. Fluctuation also provides more choices in selecting over-performers to keep and transfer into other group functions.

Nevertheless, fluctuation needs to be at least controlled and it should be foreseeable. To secure control, it is useful to have formal retention plans in place, as they can reduce the cost of fluctuation substantially. Average cost of turnover per 1000 employees was US$5.5m in companies without formal retention plans (in 2002) compared to US$3.8m for companies with formal retention plans.

TRAINING

The first fact to note about training, retention and people development cost is that in absolute terms the spending of organizations in this area is low. Training and development costs have increased by 15% between 1998 and 2001 but, regarding the total spend to hire and retain skilled professionals of US$252 per employee per year, must be deemed to be on a low level. In terms of investing in people it can actually be proven that training the employees of an SSO pays off. Comparing companies that offer 40 training hours or more per employee per year (called TFCs: training-focused centres) with those offering less than that, the results are that TFCs are better in almost every category measured (see Table 29).

Table 29   Benefits of training-focused centres

	% of centre	
	TFCs (%)	Non-TFCs (%)
Improved customer service >20	9	9
Improved process quality >20	27	12
Decreased cost >20	45	33
Improved productivity >20	55	24

TFC: Top 25% of SSOs in terms of training volume, 40+ hours per employee per year

The TFCs constitute about 25% of the SSCs and it is clear that TFCs are particularly successful in driving productivity and cost improvements. Hence, the training of SSO employees actually is an investment with a measurable positive ROI. Training should be planned and outlined by a training strategy, which includes the behaviours that should be influenced or changed, training types and content. An example of an SSO training strategy overview from a US-based hospitality company exhibits a good starting point to detail further and is shown in Figure 15.

Purpose of a training strategy	*Training strategy will include*
• Orient and acclimate associates.	• *Onboarding* – the training will consist of organizational orientation, process team introduction, benefit administration, and company policies and procedures.
• Focus on the competency model to drive behaviours and customer service quality.	• *Customer service* – the training will be implemented to ensure prompt and accurate handling of customer inquiries. This module will include telephone etiquette, assessing customer behaviour for appropriate escalation, and inquiry response (for example, within 24 hours).
• Create a multiskilled, adaptable workforce.	• *Computer skills training* – the training will consist of PC skills training, in packages such as MS Office and MS Outlook. Basic computer skills will be validated during the recruitment process.
• Create a mind-set of capturing, transferring and sharing knowledge.	• *Systems training* – the training will consist of department/unit-specific systems training, in systems such as PeopleSoft, T-RECS, FMDS and Hyperion.
• Foster peer coaching and support within the self-directed teams.	• *Hands-on training* – the training will consist of hands-on training within the process area, for all activities that are assigned to each new hire.
• Enhance career opportunities and employability.	• *Personal development training* – this training will consist of time management, conflict management resolution, self-leadership and communications.

Figure 15   SSO training strategy – example

World-class companies in general exhibit a significantly higher utilization of leadership training. World-class companies see that better-educated managers are a prerequisite for driving increased market value and therefore focus on improving their leadership qualities with 66% of the total training time being on leadership training, compared with average companies which only allocate 33% to leadership topics.

CHAPTER 6

Performance Measurement

The old saying goes: 'you cannot manage what you cannot measure'. It seems very logical that performance should be measured and that changes or improvements are difficult to communicate and validate, or even to see, if there is no way to identify them. In reality, sufficient performance measurement is still not that developed. It plays a significant role in SSOs though and it is useful to view performance measurement in connection with service level agreements (SLAs) and pricing (see Chapter 7).

BENEFITS OF PERFORMANCE MEASUREMENT

Apart from the fact that measurement seems to be necessary if any action is to be taken at all, performance measurement actually brings measurable benefits. A comparison of measurement intensive centres (MICs), defined as centres which use five or more measurement methods, with other centres shows that MICs have been significantly more successful in using their internal process data to guide process improvement efforts. MICs have experienced higher levels of improvement in customer service, quality, cost and productivity.

Table 30 Benefits of measurement-intensive centres

	% of SSC	
	Measurement intensive centres (%)	Other centres (%)
Improved productivity >20	60	20
Decreased cost >20	50	30
Improved process quality >20	45	10
Improved customer service >20	29	3

Naturally, this is not because the other SSCs could not be measured because they don't have data available. Such cases have not even been considered and most probably would rank even worse.

MEASUREMENT CONCEPT AND REPORTING

When thinking about measuring performance, one should not start with a detailed list of KPIs but instead think first about the reasons for wanting to measure. Any performance measurement approach should be embedded into a performance measurement concept. Such a concept will review, for example:

- reasons for measurement
- recipients of measurement results
- types and forms of measurement reports
- timing and intervals in which to report.

The main reasons for wanting to measure are always the need to report results and successes and the ability to influence and change performance. Any SSO project must be able to deliver some 'quick wins' to keep the momentum and convince stakeholders about the validity of the idea and the ability to execute it. Therefore, certain stakeholders, such as the CFO or steering committee, might only be interested in high-level figures and success reports while the centre itself will need to measure performance on a much more detailed level to be able to identify the causes of performance problems.

For an SSO, such a concept in its initial overview could look like the one from a US-based hospitality company illustrated in Table 31.

Table 31   Performance measurement overview

Performance reports	Suggested number of performance measures	Reporting frequency	Key users
Balanced scorecard	5–7 per SSC	Quarterly	Steering committee
Key performance indicators	3–5 per process	Monthly	SSC and business managers
Process performance measures	1–2 per employee	Daily, weekly	Process employees and coaches
Practice and peer reviews	Similar to internal audit review to monitor compliance with policies and procedures and to review all aspects of the business	Annually	Executive management, steering committee, project managers

At the beginning and during any project and operations it is useful to set up a measurement concept and to discuss the concept with the receiving parties as well as the people who should create the measurements and the reports.

The reports and their style is mainly dependent on the recipient. While the SSO's managers might be able and willing to work with Excel sheets full of numbers, the steering committee and the customers might prefer reports with more convenient reading formats such as slides with graphs and figures complemented by the exact numbers. Also, issue detection and listing alone will not be satisfying. All recipients have a need to understand what the steps are to solve those issues, when they will happen, who will engage in solving them and what the anticipated outcome will be. A tracking of action items should be incorporated into the reports.

MEASUREMENT SELECTION

It is important to draft some general guidelines on how to select the methods and the individual KPIs. Traditional measurement methods included time measurement, where individual activities would be timed by someone actually standing next to the person performing that activity. While this might still be interesting in certain areas of production, in an F&A SSO this method would be far too costly and it would be necessary to measure quite often to ensure a statistically valid result. In SSOs most measurements should be automated and can be automated. IT tools today provide a range of possibilities to retrieve data from the systems and that data can be combined intelligently into useful KPIs.

As a general guideline, measurements should fulfil the following generic criteria:

- few in number
- easy to collect (out of common systems)
- existing (available for comparison to previous)
- easy to understand.

FEW IN NUMBER

The biggest mistake made by most companies is that they define literally hundreds of KPIs. While most organizations have few measurements in place when they start with SSO, the introduction of SSO leads to exorbitant demands on information, especially by the service recipients followed by untamed creativity of the measurement providers trying to satisfy all those requirements. The result will not be helpful, as too much time is consumed in setting up the KPIs and explaining them. Also, a huge list of numbers can turn into a data graveyard and the information about actual developments, issues and solutions is hard to see. While there is no one right number of KPIs, the general rule is to try to restrict the number to a minimum.

EASY TO COLLECT

As mentioned above, KPIs should be set up using automation as much as possible. It is not useful to take the resources freed up by efficiency gains from the introduction of SSO and then employ these resources to measure what the now smaller team is doing. While measurement is necessary, the optimization gains should not be wasted on manual calculations. ERP systems provide a range of possibilities here. In some cases, such as 'incoming invoices backlog', it might be necessary actually to count manually the invoices still not booked, but such measurements should only be necessary in an initial project phase. During this time some additional resources, similar to the hockey-stick effect (see Chapter 3), will be useful, but not on a permanent basis. The measurement concept should be detailed by individual KPIs to exhibit precisely what system the data can be extracted from and what steps are necessary to get it, for example programming of queries.

EXISTING

KPIs defined in the KPI model can be as good as possible, but nearly always they cannot fulfil one important criterion. They are not available for the past. While for some this might not seem important or they would argue it cannot be changed, it is worth tackling both points.

KPIs for the past are important for comparison reasons. As mentioned in the description of the hockey-stick effect, it is vital in the initial project phase to be able to prove that the SSO is performing well, or at least that quality has only reduced within acceptable limits and only due to a short-term implementation effect. In this phase the whole project can collapse if emotional discussions about the 'better past' take over. While actual performance could possibly be proven, the comparison question remains and will be seen very differently by those affected by the changes. The only real solution, apart from ruling out discussions or using hierarchy to 'shut up' people, is to provide that comparison with past data.

In case that data were actually not available, and they hardly ever are, they can in some cases be recalculated for the past. It can be a significant effort, but if combined with the baseline data measurement activities in the initial phases of the project, the work can be streamlined significantly and this effort will certainly pay off.

In any case, it is advisable to start with collecting all existing KPIs, even if they were not measured throughout the company, and to evaluate whether those definitions could be used also in the future. In most cases the definitions created by the company itself are very useful for the internal comparison over time. They don't match external comparison requirements and therefore need to be complemented by other KPIs.

EASY TO UNDERSTAND

While there are numerous KPIs available, each one selected should be understood easily by the reporting as well as the receiving side. Simple relation figures based on two measurement components are best, for example errors in a percentage of invoices, invoices per FTE, and so on. Calculating the economic value added (EVA), IIR or NPV of the SSO might be very interesting but, at least in the first years of the SSO, hardly useful (this does not mean that the project success should not be tracked, even by IIR or NPV).

A final KPI selection and definition should be based on an evaluation of the criteria above and selection thereafter. Another key variable to consider is the targets and their priorities. In most cases KPI can be categorized into three groups, based on what they measure:

- cost and quantity
- quality
- time (or speed).

If cost is the main goal, cost-based KPIs should definitely be included and possibly have a higher weight in terms of their number relative to other KPIs. The selection of individual KPIs can also be different by process. In AR, the focus could be more on cost and quality issues, less on time (see Figure 16).

In general accounting, specifically the closing process, time might be the only really important target. Even if a company is not targeted by SARBOX, the markets and the stakeholders will demand reporting in very short time intervals and leave little time for execution. In closing, it is sometimes more important to be 'on time' than to reduce another FTE. Naturally, in SSO, cost and quality of closing would also be measured but the weighting of the KPI selection in accordance to the targets is essential to fulfil expectations.

Management-level KPIs would be more high level. Even if the final reporting format will be colourful and easy to read, an initial selection of KPIs to report to the CFO could look similar to the example of a consumer-goods company in Figure 17.

In any KPI model, it is essential to define what type of comparison will be necessary. The comparisons are always benchmarking style and can be carried out:

Selected KPIs   Ex   Int

Cost	
• Total A/R cost as a % of revenue	X
• Cost per invoice	X
• Cost per payment received	X
• Write-offs in % of sales	X
• Cost of dunning per customer	(X) X
• Cost of credit check per customer	(X) X

Quality	
• Number of invoices per FTE	X
• Number of blocked records per block type	X
• Number of invoice errors per error type	X
• Number of credit note/debit note per (error) reason	X
• Number of open unit differences on month end	X
• Number of payments per FTE	X
• Number mismatches (errors) in % of payments	X
• Number of active vendor accounts per FTE	X

Ex: external comparison

Int: internal comparison

X: available and useful

(X) available

Figure 16   KPI – accounts receivable

- externally: benchmark with other companies

- internally: benchmark between entities, business units or similar within the group

- over time: compare development (for example, once a year) with external or internal indicators.

When defining a KPI model, the solution will mostly have to incorporate KPIs available externally as well as KPIs that are only useful internally, but possibly critical to that company's measurement approach because of specific process types or the general business the company is in.

CUSTOMER SATISFACTION SURVEYS

The most difficult part of the performance measurement is the qualitative part. Here, the 'negative' quality metrics are more easy: errors, deadlines not kept, and so on. The degree of overall performance in terms of quality can be measured as a sum of different KPIs but their prioritization is somewhat subjective so the result is

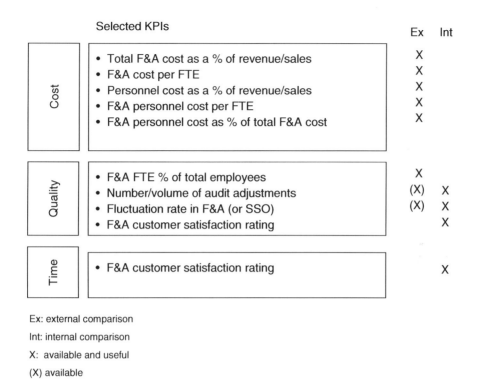

Selected KPIs

	Ex	Int
Cost		
• Total F&A cost as a % of revenue/sales	X	
• F&A cost per FTE	X	
• Personnel cost as a % of revenue/sales	X	
• F&A personnel cost per FTE	X	
• F&A personnel cost as % of total F&A cost	X	
Quality		
• F&A FTE % of total employees	X	
• Number/volume of audit adjustments	(X)	X
• Fluctuation rate in F&A (or SSO)	(X)	X
• F&A customer satisfaction rating		X
Time		
• F&A customer satisfaction rating		X

Ex: external comparison

Int: internal comparison

X: available and useful

(X) available

Figure 17   KPI – overall (management KPI)

manipulative. The SSO management might well look at a range of KPIs and assume that the total performance is excellent. However, the recipient of the service, the customer, might have a totally different view. That could be because of differing expectation levels, lack of expectation management or the failure on the SSO's part actually to find out what the customers want and how important the individual expectations actually are. The only useful way to find out is to ask. Any performance measurement approach should result in a KPI model where a customer satisfaction survey (CSS) is an integral piece of the total. A CSS in general is not difficult to perform, but there are a lot of practicalities to solve.

The first issue is to get the CSS approved. Traditionally, F&A departments have not asked their customers what they wanted. Therefore there is often a reluctance to start with that, as it is assumed that the expectations of the customers then will grow. That will probably happen initially, but the SSO concept is built on service delivery not back-office caretaking. The customers will come forward with their issues anyway, the question is just whether you want to wait for them to confront you with their demands or whether you prefer proactively to steer them. The acceptance of the new service provision will increase substantially when the clients are involved in the process.

The CSS as such can have very different formats and sizes. It is advisable to adhere to the general rules of any CSS and keep them lean, easy to understand and easy to fill out. Initially it is useful to go through the questions with the recipients, possibly even to document results for them. It should be evaluated first, however, whether that approach would influence them in their replies. The questions should be closed questions to simplify the process of consolidating and evaluating results. An open section for comments should be included to give the respondents a chance to voice comments additionally. These comments also need to be evaluated and built into the results. The presentation of results is performed mostly by trying to rate or scale the results. Scales from 0 to 4 or from 1 to 5, where 5 is the best result, have become frequent. The actual numbering system should consider, say, cultural backgrounds, what grades are used and whether a small or big number is normally good. Also, a range with an uneven number of possibilities, such as 1 to 5, has the disadvantage that respondents tend to choose the middle more often. The CSS can be performed over the Internet and should be easy to use, perhaps with drop-down menus for selection alternatives. Overall, the methodology should stay the same over time. The most important criterion is that respondents need to get feedback on their responses, both in terms of the result itself and in the form of actions from the SSO to do something about the results. Otherwise the CSS will not be interesting for the customers and they will not invest their efforts again to complete it.

CHAPTER 7

Service Pricing and Service Level Agreements

PRICING FUNDAMENTALS

The pricing of services provided by an SSO originally was not thought to be a big issue. Most SSOs used allocation methods in the beginning of their lives, exactly as they used to do in their old back-office environments. Somewhat increased transparency of services led to more demands by the customers to discuss prices. Customers wanted also to benefit from increased efficiency. The SSOs that were successful in implementing a more service-oriented working culture simultaneously realized that, by introducing a more differentiated pricing of services, it was possible to drive cross-functional performance and reduce work with low added value. A wide range of pricing ideas developed.

Today more complex discussions about how to price services are quite standard. Even though pure cost-allocation methods still make up the majority of pricing methods, the more differentiated pricing approaches are taking over and will increase further in the future. Today, in Europe, 63% of companies have some sort of cost-allocation methods included in their SLA.

The base of SLA pricing in Europe is:

- cost allocation (50%) and cost plus (13%)
- service/product-based pricing (47%)
- time-based pricing (27%)
- benchmarking (27%).

However, pricing methods also change over time. Only 33% of European companies have pricing solutions that tend to be fixed over time. Two thirds of the companies adapt their pricing methods to the changing requirements.

Before any detailed pricing KPIs are discussed, it is always advisable to think about the fundamentals of the pricing first. As a baseline, it is good to know that most companies start with a more allocation-oriented approach and change over time to more detailed pricing. An SSO often is given the target to reach some kind of 'market level' in its servicing and pricing within a specified time, perhaps between one and three years. During this time period it can be useful to stick to the previous allocation methods or use somewhat adapted allocation methods as a transfer solution. It can be beneficial to sell the SSO idea to the customer by promising, for example, a 10% reduction in costs. As a result, a pure cost allocation with 10% reduced amounts might be exactly what the customer wants, and gives the SSO some time to organize measurement and pricing for a later stage. A more progressive approach is always admirable and desirable. It must, however, be feasible in terms of culture and resources.

In any case, the fundamentals of pricing should consider a list of factors, for example:

- *Simple:* the methodology to calculate the charges must be simple to understand and require low overhead to execute.

- *Choice:* service offerings for the internal customer should reflect a choice in selecting the level of service to be provided by the SSO.

- *Fair:* costs that can be easily identified to a particular customer should be charged direct; other costs should be charged based on real-time cost drivers with incentives for desired behaviours.

- *Customer-focused:* SSO customers should 'buy-in' to pricing methodology.

- *Cost reduction:* the SSO and the SSO customer should clearly understand the opportunities to reduce cost. The cost drivers should be clear and information should be transparent and optimally displayed, perhaps using score cards.

In summary, the actual value of the pricing is defined by benefits minus costs, so the depth of the measurement and pricing should not eat up more resources than the benefits can carry.

PRICING OPTIONS

Based on targets, a clear timing of cost-allocation methods to be used and the adherence to pricing fundamentals, the next step is to list the pricing options available to choose from. There are numerous thinkable options, but the main pricing options include:

- *No allocation:* costs remain in SSOs. This method is also used in cases where customer service usage is unchanged or no ability to change customer behaviour is expected.

- *Costs allocated to corporate:* the corporate then (possibly) reallocates. It is a simple process to distribute costs outside the SSO. However, this method does not provide the ability to use pricing as a method of modifying customer behaviour.

- *Actual cost allocation:* this is a simple method of allocating actual costs to customers based on drivers such as number of employees or percentage of total revenue. Typically this method is used by a newly opened SSO where little information about current cost structures or cost drivers is known. It is also used by SSOs undergoing extensive process re-engineering efforts. Measurement efforts can sometimes be significant.

- *Fixed-allocation amount:* this is similar to actual-cost allocation but amount charged is agreed up-front in the budgeting process regardless of actual results. It is advantageous for the SSO if the SSO is more efficient than planned, a disadvantage if the centre is unable to influence behaviours of their customers in other ways.

- *Transaction-based pricing:* this method is typically used by more established SSOs and/or those with a good understanding of their own cost structures. It is also used by SSOs when cost reduction is a predominant goal of the company. Prices can be based on planned SSO costs, actual cost or predetermined benchmark objectives.

- *Fixed pricing:* this includes a cost per transaction that is fixed and not impacted by volume shifts. The SSO's staffing levels and cost structures could have an effect on financial results. Typically, a proper blend of supplemental labour (such as temps) are utilized to reduce the risk.

- *Volume-based pricing:* variable cost per transaction based on the number of transactions processed by the SSO. Prices are set by volume tier. The main advantage of this approach is that the customer either benefits or is penalized financially based on the number of transactions being processed by the SSO on their behalf. Additionally, the risk of not being able to pass on all costs incurred by the SSO is greatly diminished when the tiered pricing structure is properly set up.

- *Menu-based pricing:* in this method, pricing is carried out regardless of actual results of SSO. As service centres mature, this option is becoming very popular. Prices are based on actual service volume rendered to the customer. Exception pricing is included to discourage customer behaviour which has a negative impact on SSO efficiency levels or process improvement initiatives. Menu-based pricing also provides visibility to the services provided by the SSO.

It is possible to combine different methods and they will change over the course of time anyway, but keep in mind the fundamentals: keep it simple.

The decision-making process for selecting the pricing methods and drivers can be quite lengthy if too much discussion is involved. A way to speed up the discussion is to provide a decision tree which helps link the targets, service types and pricing methods and at least reduces the amount of options to the useful and suitable ones (see Figure 18).

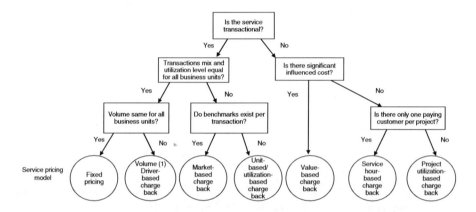

Figure 18   Service pricing model framework – decision tree

The questions in the decision tree are always similar but the outcome obviously can vary by company. The pricing fundamentals, again, should not be forgotten when evaluating the results.

TRENDS IN SERVICE PRICING

The main reason to price services naturally is to recover costs by charging the customers, for example business units. Apart from trying to 'get rid of the costs', there are several other reasons for the SSO to use cost allocation or pricing. For one, the pricing can be an efficient method to influence customer behaviour (see Table 33). More and more companies acknowledge that pricing services in a specific way can be used to change the service mix required. Expensive and little value-adding services, such as reports produced as a standard process to everybody, can be priced artificially high to force the customer to think about whether they really require this report. Lowering the price for the same service over time makes the customer understand better the necessity to discuss the service provision process and the customer's duties, such as delivering concise data to be processed. The benefit will help the customer understand that the optimization together with the SSO actually delivers a benefit.

Table 32   Cost recovery by existing SSO

	% of companies
Completed implementation	60
In process of implementation	20
Evaluating the idea	2
Idea has not been considered	2
Decision not to implement	14
Attempted and failed	2

Note: 82% of centres said that cost recovery was either a critical component of their vision, or consistent with it

Table 33   Customer behaviour influencing pricing in existing SSO

	% of companies
Critical component of vision	11
Consistent with vision	59
Not a component of vision	25
Inconsistent with corporate culture	5

Note: 70% of centres said that charging business units to influence customers was either a critical component of their vision, or consistent with it

As the trends in service pricing show (see Table 34), there is also a move from purely internal methods to a more market-oriented view. It can be a positive result for a company if the new SSO is able to reduce costs every year, but the potential available is largely dependent on the starting position. If the company was extremely expensive in the first place, the improvements might only be marginal, compared to what other companies pay for similar services or compared to actually available external services. Hence, the comparison with external methods is becoming a key component in pricing strategies.

Table 34   Trends in service pricing

	% of companies	
	2000	*2003*
Predetermined/fixed rates or amount	73	41
Variable rate based on actual volumes	43	55*
Rate based on benchmarks	9	20*

*Utilization of the predetermined rate will shift significantly to the other two methodologies.

The move from fixed rates to more variable pricing is one that can be attributed to the maturing of SSOs. The trend to benchmark externally is proof of the growing insight within most companies that a service that is regarded non-core, and hence provided by an internal service unit, over time must be also comparable with external service levels and prices. For some areas there are external service providers in the market and the price comparison can be done against actual external offers; for other areas, a comparison with the internal pricing of similar companies might still be useful. Offers from business process outsourcing (BPO) can be a good way to validate the cost of the complete service package.

Table 35   Utilization of menu pricing in 2000 and 2003

	% of companies	
	2000	*2003*
Completed implementation	11	27*
In process of implementation	11	7
Evaluating the idea	20	34*
Idea has not been considered	14	14
Decision not to implement	43	18
Attempted and failed	–	–

*Utilization of menu pricing for SSC increases significantly as centre matures.

Menu-based pricing is maybe the most advanced of the current methods used (see Table 35). Its usage is to grow substantially over the next years. If menu-based pricing is understood as a target to reach, the road through the different pricing options can be quite successful.

SERVICE LEVEL AGREEMENTS

A service level agreement (SLA) is one of those components of an SSO that originally had a limited visibility and now has become one of the most talked-about topics. An SLA actually is a very important tool in effectively managing an SSO. Nevertheless, the biggest mistake often made is to start discussing SLAs in a much too early phase. Often companies ask for examples of SLAs when they are in the planning stages. First of all, the examples can be interesting but seldom are useful – they cannot be simply copied. And the SLA really is only needed when the feasibility work is done and the design is underway or completed.

In general, an SLA is a type of contractual agreement between the service provider and the customer. The usage or significance of an SLA is largely independent of the fact that the SSO is organized as a separate legal entity or not. In case it is, the contract will be legally required; if not, the SLA is still required based on business needs. In both cases, the content will have to be discussed – the transfer price level, for instance. The SLA in general specifies the service scope, service level and the pricing and can include a range of other topics. A typical SLA would include components such as:

- *Scope and description of services provided:* as comprehensive as possible list of services and of process cut-over points, links and interfaces.

- *Customer-service delivery description:* an outline of how the provider organization will service the customer, specifically detailing the contact persons for services, hours of availability and communication tools to be used.

- *Cost information:* a description of the pricing or proposed charges for services provided. This will increase transparency, clearly specify cost drivers and possibly break down charges on a service-by-service basis.

- *External benchmarks:* a comparison of current performance services levels and cost against external benchmarks (to be updated regularly).

- *Performance-level commitments:* commitments by the provider based on KPIs and possibly in summary as a percentage of customer satisfaction or a percentage of total service level compared to previous state.

- *Customer commitment:* a comprehensive outline of customer requirements that will enable the provider to meet specified performance-level commitments, for instance the customer's duties in delivering data, informing the SSO about issues or changes, validating and answering questions within a specified time window (validating the correctness of invoices without purchase orders or validating receipt of goods and services for matching).

- *Process improvement:* a description of process improvement initiatives to be undertaken by the provider, by the customer or jointly, for the term of the agreement, and the expected benefits associated with these improvements.

- *Issue resolution:* an outline of how issues and disagreements will be resolved between the provider and the customer with escalation procedures and time-lines.

- *Terms:* the length of time over which the agreement is enforced and possibly description of process to discuss (dis)continuation.

Naturally the SLA can include more topics or just some of those listed above. That is because every SLA is different and has to be, since the SLA is set up in accordance to the needs it should help satisfy. In Europe in 2003, companies mostly had process descriptions and KPIs included in their SLAs:

1. Process description (71%).

2. KPI for performance measurement (71%).

3. Pricing (67%).

4. Hours of operation (51%).

5. Information about contact persons (49%).

6. Guidelines for escalation proceedings; that is, arbitration and so on (40%).

7. Other (2%).

On a global basis, in 2002, 55% of companies had SLAs with their customers. In Europe in 2003, 78% of companies used SLAs. Hardly any company today implements an SSO without setting up an SLA. As described above, the content differs significantly. Just in terms of the number of pages in an SLA it is clear that the content must be very different, at least in terms of level of detail (see Table 36).

Table 36   Number of pages in SLA

1–5 pages	28%
6–15 pages	21%
16–25 pages	21%
26–50 pages	15%
More than 50 pages	15%

In terms of necessary detail, there are differing views on how detailed an SLA should be. Some companies, HP for example, report having SLAs with just a few pages. The idea behind this is based mainly on the type of general company culture. HP wanted to enforce significant interaction between the SSO and the customer. This way, both sides would get a better understanding of the full process and the other party's needs and issues.

An SLA really is an important change management tool in the sense that it brings together both sides, and people involved in the process will better adapt to the mind-set of providing and receiving services: being in a service environment instead of a back-office. Specifically, the SLA discussion process facilitates change in the following areas:

- Service providers will have a better understanding of business needs and will be able to incorporate business requirements and desired service levels into process improvement initiatives.

- Businesses/customers will have a better understanding of the cost drivers of the services offered.

- Businesses/customers will have a deeper knowledge base to determine what their service needs are and a better understanding of how specific services add value to their business.

A German-based retailer in turn set up a very detailed SLA based on the scepticism of some SSO customers in the concept itself and in the SSO's ability to deliver the necessary services while keeping within previous quality levels. In this case, the savings were guaranteed, a comprehensive set of KPIs included and even the hockey-stick effect (see Chapter 3) was incorporated. Originally, the hockey-stick effect should have been limited to a specified percentage, but there was no agreement on how to define and measure that percentage.

The detailing of SLAs clearly depends on the individual company's situation and needs, but general pros and cons are shown in Table 37, and the more detailed ones in Table 38.

Table 37 Advantages and disadvantages of a summary SLA

Advantages	Disadvantages
• Necessary information is provided in a concise format	• Does not cover all situations in detail
• Customer review and approval process are simple	• Requires a high level of trust between customer and service centre
• Maintenance is kept at a low level	
• Development and use is kept easy	

It is possible to combine some of the pros for detailed and summary SLAs by setting up a summary SLA first and then an additional operational SLA with more detail. Also, in any SLA, it makes sense to include content and parameters that can change over time (such as KPIs, names of contact persons), as separate pages in the form of appendices, so those changes will only trigger new appendices, not the necessity to rewrite the whole contract. SLA and connected pricing trends in summary include at least the following observations:

- As SSOs start off, the charge-out method is typically simple. However, as these organizations mature they find that more in-depth pricing options are required which allow them to impact customer behaviour. Established SSOs often are able to simplify SLAs again. There is something like a 'life-cycle of SLAs'.

- A current trend amongst SSOs is the inclusion of additional charges for research and development, future capital expenditures, and even a profit margin.

- The development of a service pricing strategy for the SSO is an important topic that extends well beyond simply distributing costs – it requires the strict attention of the SSO leadership to make sure that the methodology used supports the strategy of the organization.

The life-cycle of SLAs can be exhibited nicely by a case example and the respective changes in the SLA of a US-based company within a five-year period, starting with the SLA set-up:

- *Eight years ago:* initially the company set up a very detailed, formal-looking agreement (30–40 pages). Long discussions with customers were necessary – two companies did not sign.

- *Seven years ago:* it became apparent that for measurement purposes of the SSO the KPIs were OK but the business units were not interested in that level of detail.

- *Six years ago:* the company created new summary SLAs (five pages).

- *Four years ago:* since then SLAs have not been used in a formal sense. Quick-reference service guides are available on the intranet. Very few measurements are kept for SSO purposes.

Table 38   Advantages and disadvantages of a detailed SLA

Advantages	Disadvantages
● Clearly defines responsibilities and commitments	● Time-consuming to develop and secure approval
● Includes formal approach from customer	● Significant maintenance required to remain up-to-date
● Service centre develops a clear understanding of its scope	● Often too inconvenient to be utilized on a regular basis
● Effective in a controlled environment	

In summary, SLAs are essential, need to be discussed at the right time and need to be linked with performance measurement and pricing. SLAs should be set up based on the targets and company culture, not copied directly from others. Effective SSOs must have SLAs to be able to engage in structured discussions with their customers. Without SLAs, a service mind-set is hard to implement.

CHAPTER 8

The Structure of Shared Service Organizations

THE CASE OF GLOBAL SSCs

There is a number of ways to organize shared services. In addition, there is a number of different topics to discuss under the topic of organization, for example the organization of the SSO as a whole and the internal organization of one SSC. Organization also relates to the governance of the SSO and to questions around using process owners and the service scope of an individual SSC. Lastly, one should not forget that there will remain a local organization, which also should be covered.

Many companies are aspiring to set up one global SSC. However, none has been able to reach that state until today. The logic behind wanting to set up one global SSC is that if there is one optimal site that can be or has been chosen as the SSC site, and if all services globally could be performed from this one SSC, then the benefits should be the greatest. It is imaginable that someone will reach this state, but practically it does not necessarily make sense. Let's take a very successful SSO example to discuss: HP.

HP has one internal global SSC in Bangalore, India. However, HP also has three regional SSCs in Europe, Asia and North America. These SSCs provide services that cannot (or could not so far) be provided on a global basis because of the different regional or country-specific requirements. HP also has an outsourcing deal as a back-up solution, in case one of the SSCs breaks down, for example. Apart from the fact that these centres do not always cover 100% of process content, entities and countries, the solution in total is very advanced. The question now is whether there actually will be benefits in closing down the three regional SSCs and moving those activities into the SSC in India. Whatever the internal answer of HP might be, it seems that for a range of reasons a global SSO is both possible and beneficial; however, it is questionable whether that one global SSO should be built out of just one global SSC. Even in a very advanced solution, where a global SSC might perform a significant amount of the total services, it seems to be the case that some parts of the processes or sub-processes in total must be left either in the country or in the region. If one should now try, as in the HP example, to move the content of the regional SSCs to the global SSC, it could be expected that this in turn will require some parts of the work (so far in the regional SSCs) being moved back to the countries: those parts that had to be kept at a regional level because of the problems in moving them to India in the first place. The result would therefore be just a different split of activities, where the global portion would grow but the local portion would also grow and the regional SSCs would possibly close down.

A detailed business case will certainly deliver the right answers, but in general all the existing SSOs that are very advanced are operating in an organizational structure made up of several tiers of centres and activities. It is also often said that the centre size should not grow too big, because that would make it more difficult to manage the SSO and it would eat up some benefits. A global SSO today will involve global, but also regional and local, activities. The amount of levels can be even greater. The goal of one global SSC is a useful one to have in terms of vision, and it might be possible to achieve in the future, if for example legal and regulatory environments globally become more unified and if risk aspects allow it.

For our organization discussion, it should be noted that one global SSO will exist of several SSCs as there are some processes that until today have not been successfully migrated onto the global level. The overview presented in Figure 19 exhibits what geographical level is the highest that, based on existing SSC scopes today, can be used to perform certain F&A processes.

	Business partnering	Controlling	Payroll	VAT	Collections	Billing	Closing	Statutory reporting	Accounts payable	Accounts receivable	Fixed assets	Intercompany
Site	X											
National		X	X	X								
Regional					X	X	X	X				
Global									X	X	X	X

Figure 19 The case for global shared services

This overview will most probably change over time, but even so it is difficult to imagine how business partnering or total control could be performed on a global basis. Of course, if a company has a defined SSO scope of only AP, AR, intercompany (IC) and fixed assets (FA), then the answer could well be that inside that scope one global SSC is possible. And, of course, 'more' might be possible in its purest sense, but if the solution makes no sense economically, for example, or cannot deliver sustainable quality service, it should not be considered possible or practicable.

Most companies, though, are still fighting with the move from local activities to national consolidation or from national SSCs to regional SSCs. An overview of European companies, which is most informative in terms of regions because of the large differences within Europe, exhibits that 60% have some regional activities and only 5% have managed to actually move parts of the process scope to a global platform (see Table 39).

Table 39   Geographical scope of shared services unit(s)

Regional SSC (for several countries)	60%
National SSC (for one country)	52%
Outsourced (serviced by an external provider)	10%
Global SSC (all countries)	5%
Joint venture (internal, but with an external partner)	0%

Note: Multiple answers possible

ORGANIZATIONAL ALTERNATIVES

The organization discussion should always start by defining the operating model first. Based on this, an organizational discussion is possible and useful. There is a range of dimensions to discuss or define what type of SSO should be created, but the most important ones are:

- geography
- business scope (business unit/division)
- functional alignment.

Geography

Obviously the geography is one dimension that always comes up first and hence has been discussed briefly above in terms of the ultimate goal. In general the potential geographical models include:

- *Local:* keep activities local (where they are).
- *National:* group activities by country.
- *Regional:* group activities by region or sub-region (here: several countries, for instance Benelux, Scandinavia, Europe, North America, South-East Asia, Greater China).
- *Global:* all activities globally.

As listed above, the geographical view can be divided in different ways. It is also possible to define other geographies, such as regions within one country, as the relevant scope. The criterion in reality is not really the geography but assumed differences and commonalities between and amongst geographies, where the chosen geographical term is assumed to represent these quite well as a summary criterion.

Also, the geographical scope might differ depending on the content. A pan-European solution or a regional solution might incorporate different countries, say, for a competence centre compared with a transactional centre. A centre of excellence has different location criteria to a transactional centre and hence might be in a different location, even if the geographical scope is similar or equal. A geography, even if defined, could also be organized based on a virtual solution. The geographical scope would be the same but the solution totally different in terms of the operating model.

The look at the geography often reflects the existing decision powers in a company. If Europe can run projects for Europe, than the scope automatically is defined as Europe. A regional SSC might be targeted or in existence because it was driven by a regional effort and the sponsor was simply not able to get the remaining countries to participate. Also, a regional SSC might be the result of the decision-makers of one region deciding to work against a pan-European SSC. Setting up a regional SSC might make a pan-European SSC redundant or at least move its location to that of the regional SSC. The strategy might fail too, but is still used quite often in Europe as a means to keep as much control as possible. Ultimately, organizational decisions are mostly power decisions and very often do not reflect economic criteria.

Business scope

Another relevant dimension is the one dealing with the service recipients and their scope. Who should the SSO service: the whole corporation, or should individual businesses within the group have their own SSO? This is a question almost more difficult to solve than the geography issue. And it is not possible to give the general answer that solves either because 'it really depends'.

The starting point for solving the issue should be:

- What is a business?
- Is our business split (in terms of business units, for instance) relevant for the service split?

Decision-makers in the company naturally go by the existing divisional or business-unit limits, regardless of the fact that content differences between the business units in terms of type of business, processes, culture and so on might sometimes be huge, sometimes non-existent. Large global groups – GE, IBM, Siemens – have so many different businesses within them that the relevant scope to look at most probably is often one of the businesses: just the telecommunication business, just the medical business or just the industrial production. Often comparisons in looking at achievements of others are done company by company: what did HP do, what did Henkel do, what did GM do? When discussing large conglomerates, the fact that the whole group has one name is, for SSO purposes, sometimes almost irrelevant. When one business inside a global conglomerate can be the market leader in its field, it should be compared to other companies in the same field, regardless of independence and ownership structures. And possibly the right scope for discussing an SSO solution is not IBM or GE in total, but just one of their businesses, just the insurance business of GE for example. It is, of course, a benefit to be able to look at this decision from the top down and choose the best scope. Not everyone has this opportunity. The point is that it is not realistic to expect the same type of solution for very diversified conglomerates compared to homogeneous businesses, even if they all have geographical diversity.

The optimal solution could be to drive the scope search to a top-down decision, engage all relevant decision-makers regardless of where the initiative started and then choose project and SSO scopes as necessary. Often this is not done. Instead, depending on existing steering and measurement criteria, each SSO sponsor looks at his or her responsibility area and defines the SSO scope accordingly. The result is often a 'bottom-up' road map in terms of SSO evolution. An example of a typical evolutionary approach could be IBM and its HR service centre history:

- pre-1992: local consolidations
- 1992: US regionalization
- 1995: US centralization
- 1998: multi-country support in Europe
- 2000: global.

Even if this is based on the HR SSO, the development has been similar to a number of companies and it is often the only possible way.

It is advisable to go through the scoping exercise as a part of implementing the SSO on a decision-making level as high as possible (for instance, the group CFO/FD, the group CEO/MD) and base it on carefully defined SSO-scoping criteria that are as independent of current business-unit limits as possible.

Functional alignment

The functional alignment dimension is a third important point. It is similar to the business-unit discussion and sometimes the definition or wording can actually be exactly opposite; or functional alignment can include both aspects. Here, functional alignment is mainly about whether the SSO is purely a finance SSO or whether it also serves other functions, such as HR.

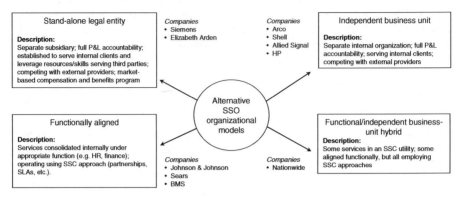

Figure 20   Four typical SSO organizational models

This is such a big field that we will look at detailed topics below, but, as an overview, organizational models could be split into four basic categories as shown in Figure 20. These four types of organizations may have been developed or chosen due to different reasons but often they also reflect the origin of the company. Shared services are useful both for companies coming from very decentralized, possibly divisional structures, as well as those wanting to become more service-oriented, often originating from large centralized functions. Both ways lead to one of the four models, however:

- Companies that originate in very decentralized structures often have very limited process and functional scope but are very process-oriented and efficient.

- Companies originating in large corporate structures can include large scopes by top-down decision-making but have difficulties in clear process orientation.

- Cross-functional companies seem to be more dependent on individual culture.

- Independent companies seem to be reliant on culture and geography.

Descriptions of the four models are generic and SSO solutions vary significantly in reality, but summaries of typical content and outcome include:

- Defined process centres:
  - Centralization to achieve scale economies with a focus on individual processes within a function (for example finance or HR).

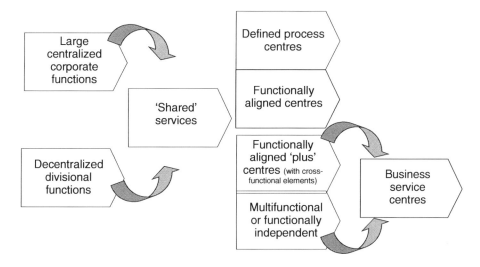

Figure 21   Approaches to shared services

  - – Improvement efforts that are internally focused with limited impact on processes that are 'upstream' or 'downstream' to centre processes.
  - – A modified model for delivering centralized processes with a focus on production excellence.
  - – Customer preference is 'invisible' and low cost – less is more.
  - – Limited impact or influence within the company or between centres.
  - – Low status (with some exceptions).

- ● Functionally aligned centres:
  - – Centralization of multiple processes to achieve scale economies with a focus on functional process excellence (for example finance or HR).
  - – A separate business entity with a defined planning and strategy development process.
  - – Impact and influence within the company varies dramatically.
  - – Customer preferences range from 'be invisible' to 'value–add resources'.
  - – Wide range in service centre status and centre independence within the company.

- ● Functionally aligned 'plus' centres (with cross-functional elements):
  - – Centralization of processes to achieve scale economies with an increased focus on end-to-end process excellence.
  - – A blurring of traditional functional boundaries with 'order-to-cash' or 'purchase-to-pay' process components in the same centre.
  - – Greater visibility and influence within the company on end-to-end process design.

– Inclusion of other functional processes in the service centre often constrained by traditional views of process affiliations.
– Implementations range from 'side by side' to 'full integration'.

● Multifunctional or functionally independent centres:
  – Centralization of processes to achieve scale economies with a strong focus on end-to-end process excellence.
  – An elimination of traditional functional boundaries with 'order-to-cash' or 'purchase-to-pay' process components in the same centre.
  – Leverage core competencies into new areas based on skills to perform activities, not on functional affiliation.
  – Greater visibility and influence within the company on end-to-end process design.
  – Change in reporting relationship does not instantly translate to increased status or multifunctional process design.

These four different organizational models are just examples of how to define different organizational solution alternatives. The list could be divided differently, say, for a discussion on the operating model. Naturally the organization models always lead to different organizational set-ups with resulting different organization charts. The basic organization chart differences could also look like those in Figures 22, 23, 24 and 25.

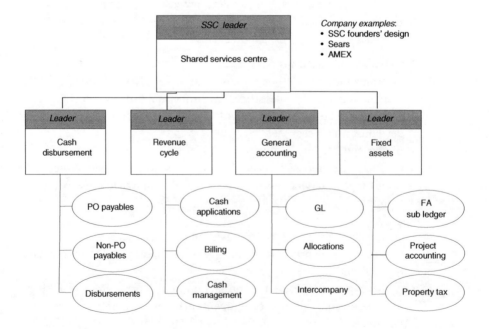

Figure 22   Detailed organizational diagrams – pure functional

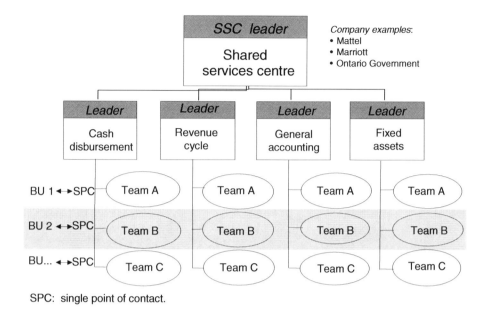

Figure 23   Detailed organizational diagrams – functional/virtual customer

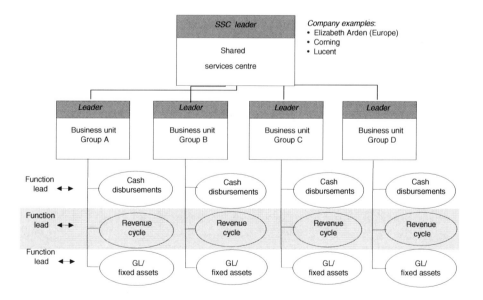

Figure 24   Detailed organizational diagrams – customer/virtual function

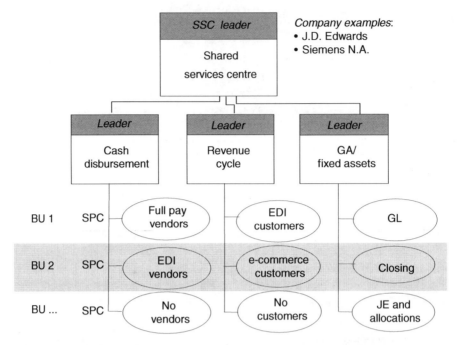

SPC: single point of contact.

Figure 25   Detailed organizational diagrams – end-to-end process

CROSS-FUNCTIONAL ORGANIZATION

The selection of a cross-functional solution is still quite unusual. In Europe, only 26% of companies have organized their SSO cross-functionally. Three quarters (or 76%) are functional, only operating within the finance function.

A cross-functional organization can be useful for several reasons:

● A transactional SSO should incorporate all transactional processes suited for the purpose. Some of the processes often categorized as HR, such as T&E and payroll, can easily be part of the same SSO as AR, AP and so on. As an example, one US consumer-goods company that already had a well-established finance SSC for Europe operational for about ten years in Dublin did not include T&E and payroll in this SSC, but instead looked for an HR SSC solution including those processes, although the other HR processes required a different set-up and the content needed to be split into different parts. The driver was the split functional responsibility. HR looked for a solution of its own and did not want to 'give away' its processes, although this might have been the right answer.

- A full-process-cycle scope, such as OTC or PTP, includes process steps within different functions. In PTP, including the incoming invoice verification in the SSO is easy as this is nearly always in the finance department, but leaving out the purchase administration, for instance, does not reflect the full-process-cycle idea. Equally, in OTC, excluding order intake and billing from the SSO, just because they are currently under the supervision of the sales department, creates holes in the process work and does not leave a lot of room for optimization. The full-process-cycle view needs to result in a cross-functional SSO structure.

- Any end-to-end view is similar to the full-process-cycle view (e.g. PTP, OTC). End-to-end must result in cross-functional organization.

Despite the benefits of organizing cross-functionally, there are difficulties in making it happen. These 'political' reasons are currently still quite dominant, exhibiting the fact that support process topics are still regarded as core business by those responsible for them or that top management in these companies cannot clearly communicate alternative uses for these individuals, resulting in protective strategies.

CENTRE INDEPENDENCE

The independence of the SSO is a very interesting topic to discuss. Some of the reasons why include:

- Centre independence has significant advantages, including the ability to break down cross-functional barriers which can help to dramatically increase the centre's scope of operation.

- There is a greater risk of an independent centre being dismantled if an acquisition occurs, since most companies utilize a more traditional structure.

- What may be an ideal structure for one shared services organization may not be appropriate for another. Any decisions in this area need to be well thought out in advance and reflect the operating model chosen, which in turn should always include a choice in terms of SSO independence.

Also, the listing of common attributes for SSO in general often includes components such as the following:

- managed like an independent business
- SLAs; negotiated service contracts
- standardized services and menu pricing

- charge-backs to customers for services (not just allocation)

- internal 'outsourcing'; customers can source elsewhere

- arm's-length relationship with customers

- leverage technology and skills expertise

- institutionalized continuous improvement approaches

- consolidation of processes to obtain scale advantages

- staff processes (not line or operations).

Many of these common attributes are directly linked to the question of centre independence, so it is also useful to find out whether we are discussing a 'real SSO' or centralization. Centre independence is low but increasing (see Table 40). Based on very comprehensive results from The Hackett Group, centre independence can be characterized as being currently as shown in Table 41. Even though only 43% of the centres are managed like independent businesses, 70% of these same centres view centre independence as critical to or consistent with their vision. Hence, we can expect more centres in the future to opt for more independence.

Table 40   Shared services overview

What companies are doing today	Implemented or are implementing (%)
Shared services is organized as a separate legal entity	17
Shared services reports to a senior business executive, not aligned functionally	16
Customers are able to select providers other than the service centre	15
Shared services includes price negotiations and competitive bidding	32
Shared services has a business development manager position(s)	22

Table 41   Extent to which SSCs are managed like independent businesses

Completed and implemented	43%
Implementation in process	25%
Evaluating the idea	10%
Idea not considered	10%
Decided no or attempted and failed	12%

Table 42   Extent to which SSCs are separate and distinct from corporate HQ

Completed and implemented	63%
Implementation in process	14%
Evaluating the idea	8%
Idea not considered	8%
Decided no or attempted and failed	7%

Sixty-three per cent of SSCs are separated and distinct from headquarters (see Table 42). This is a significant figure, although detailed results show that this distinction is much greater in North America than in other regions, like Europe, where it is still the minority.

Table 43   Extent to which SSC is responsible for defining company policy for processes

Completed and implemented	54%
Implementation in process	26%
Evaluating the idea	4%
Idea not considered	4%
Attempted and failed	12%

In 54% of cases the SSO defines corporate policies for processes (see Table 43). The extent to which a service centre is responsible for defining company policy in general would be difficult to measure, as the overall policy definition should not be included in a transactional SSO, but instead in competence centres or HQ. But, in terms of processes, the SSO, even the individual SSC, should actively participate and lead the process of defining policies. Hence 54% is a good result in terms of independence, but substantially short of the 78% actually defining this as critical to or consistent with their vision.

Table 44   Extent to which SSCs have pay levels specific to shared services

Completed and implemented	31%
Implementation in process	8%
Evaluating the idea	8%
Idea not considered	18%
Attempted and failed	35%

A very relevant measurement is the extent to which SSCs have pay levels specific to the SSO (see Table 44), and hence different to the remaining organization. One of the main drivers for SSOs is the cost advantage of shared services, perhaps because of a different location. As a result, the pay levels would be expected to be very different. In reality, only 31% report successful implementation of different pay levels; 35% on the contrary report having failed in trying to do so or having decided against trying.

This is quite extraordinary, because it exhibits one of the most difficult issues to solve. An SSO should have freedom to decide on its own pay level in order to achieve its goals. In reality, this decision power is restricted by company culture, unionized contracts, workers' council triggering compromises in the implementation process, salary guarantees to 'buy' support of individuals and so on.

The independence figures are significantly lower when we have a look at Europe, and then lower still when we stay in one country. It is almost impossible to set up a national SSO and in doing so to get out of the existing pay scheme agreed upon (for example within a union). On the other hand, this is one of the main reasons why implementing SSOs in Europe (as well as in parts of Asia and South America) is so much more difficult than in North America. A new structure for an SSO in Europe is difficult enough to build, but it is even more difficult to move to different pay schemes, even if the new organization is a different legal entity. Good business and legal advice is necessary here.

In summary, the view on organizational independence tells us that different companies have taken different routes and that organizational independence, whether actual or desired, is a main driver for organizational decision-making about the SSO. One of the results to remember in this context is that it seems to be easier to arrive at cross-functional solutions, include a larger process scope in the SSO and have greater independence, when decision-making is on the highest level – at CEO level instead of CFO level, for instance. Also, organizational independence bears a greater risk (or chance) of change, such as being dismantled again later.

INDIVIDUAL SSC SCOPE AND ORGANIZATION

Apart from the question about how to organize the SSO overall, another relevant view on the SSO structure is the question of how to organize one SSC. The 'internal' SSC organization might not seem to be a big issue, but there are alternative ways to choose from. In Europe, 70% of companies have decided to organize 'by process'. This means that the individual SSC has teams or groups of people that belong together because of the process knowledge they share and the process activities they work on. An alternative would be to organize by countries (done by 29%) with a 'one face to the country' philosophy, or to organize by business units (17%).

Each way has advantages and disadvantages. Companies which believe that the country specifics are huge, and hence have difficulties moving to a standard platform, often tend to think of country-specific organization as the logical thing to do. Also, language issues might require native speakers per country for certain activities, making country-specific organization more attractive.

In reality, there is always a country and a process dimension to the organization within the SSC. The question is only which one is dominant. Experience shows that the best solution is to start with the process orientation because, although more difficult in the beginning, it helps to standardize processes across the scope faster than the country organization. The fact that all AP service people sit together in one room in the SSC helps them discuss and find solutions and standardize faster than if they coordinate primarily with other processes for the same client.

There is something like a life cycle for the SSC organization. After standardizing processes successfully across the scope, say across Europe, the organization can be changed again to country organization. This has been done by some companies, Whirlpool for example. When standardization reached a very high degree, the benefits of serving a country or entity as the primary focus become more dominant than the necessity of further standardizing.

As a result, the organization solution should always 'follow the difficult path in order to reach the goals faster'; in other words, to start with process orientation and move to country organization after having successfully standardized. This road map is supported by the fact that basically all SSOs organize by teams with flat hierarchies (in Europe 91%) so the team structure is the common platform.

Organization by business units/divisions is a solution mostly chosen by those companies that have opted to provide services from one SSO to several different businesses. These are normally those large conglomerates discussed above, that could easily have specific SSOs even per business. If they do try for a cross-business SSO, than it is quite logical that there will be a business focus somewhere in the organization, in this case on the lowest level; in other words, at least the SSC team organization will reflect the diversity of the group and the magnitude of the scope. These SSO solutions are often quite advanced and useful to review. Companies organizing their SSC teams by business unit/division but having no business necessity to do so, whose processes could be merged because the differences are not substantial, are on the contrary not recommended as examples. Since 99% organize by process or country, the business-unit organization seems to be only an additional organization layer, probably only relevant for the conglomerate candidates.

PROCESS ORGANIZATION

We have discussed how important processes are and how all SSO work is linked to processes. Also, we have discussed process orientation in the team set-up within an SSC. Many would think that we have covered the topic of process organization already but process organization is actually much more than process orientation. Process orientation is the process view on team level built into a normal functional organization, whereas a process organization is an organization where the solid reporting line is on the processes and which reflects a functional organization flipped by 90 degrees to make the horizontal process view the vertical or main organization view (see Figure 26).

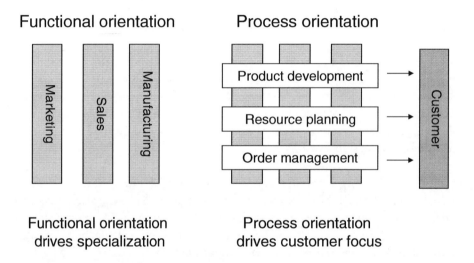

Figure 26   Process orientation versus functional orientation

Without wanting to go into theoretical depths, here is a brief recap on processes and functions:

What is a PROCESS?

A business process is the sum of related tasks and activities flowing through an organization, not limited to a single function or department, by which an output is produced. Processes define both how a business operates and the way in which it delivers value to its customers. Processes involve both manual (human) and automated (systems) activities and hence are not purely the sum of IT functionalities. Integrating all activities into a seamless flow producing required outputs provides process excellence and competitive advantage.

A process provides value to its stakeholders (customers, shareholders and employees) through the outcomes it produces. In process design, it is critical to first define the value that will be delivered by the process – the output and its use – and then focus on this when designing the process changes. Redesign is only valuable when it helps change outcomes in a way that will create substantial value.

What is a FUNCTIONAL ORGANIZATION?

Most organizations manage their business through a functional organization made of functional departments. Typical business functions include core functions, such as sales, manufacturing and research and development and support functions, that could comprise accounting, purchasing, IT and HR. In a functionally oriented organization, an employee's work is narrowly defined by what is done; by the activity itself, not by the overall outcome.

This concept originated from Adam Smith's idea of breaking work into its simplest tasks and having a specialist perform each. Departmental structures evolved to manage these tasks, with vertical reporting relationships to the head of the department. Often, employees lost sight of the real objectives or process outcomes, such as delivering product to the customer. In a functional structure, work often passes sequentially through departmental hand-offs, each with its own checks and controls, resulting in double-work.

Functionally oriented organizations have often been referred to as 'silo' organizations. The silo metaphor is used because business activities are focused upward, towards functional management, instead of outward, towards internal or external customers. Skill development, performance measurements and promotions are also focused upward within the silo.

The process orientation, in contrast to functional orientation, represents a complete shift in thinking. It aligns tasks and activities to achieve outcomes valued by a customer, whether internal or external. Under a process orientation, goal-oriented process teams consist of people from all participating functions, whether it is one or many. Activities often occur in parallel, rather than sequentially, with frequent integration points. The organization is aligned by the processes, horizontally as well as vertically, and by function, producing a matrix with the main lines running in accordance with the process view. A process orientation fosters flexibility and change readiness. When outcomes change, for example, process-oriented teams find it easier to modify their activities in response.

An organization must understand what it does best to achieve the proper balance between process and functional orientations. Different areas of the organization might have varying degrees of process orientation. For instance, customer service operations may be more process-oriented because of their heavy customer emphasis than, for example, financial activities.

Process organization is the next step from process orientation – and it is truly revolutionary. Not many companies have managed actually to change the organization set-up to reflect the importance of the process view; however, it is the logical consequence of process orientation. We expect more companies to move through matrix organization as the intermediate step to a process organization, often run by people called process owners (sometimes shortened 'PO' – not to be confused with purchase order!).

It only makes sense to consider a change if there is a benefit linked to it. Let's summarize the key aspects of a process organization in terms of the question: 'Do we need it?'

- Process organization is a more complex organization form than functional organization and requires higher skill levels offering a more sophisticated work environment.

- Process organization does not mean the abolition of vertical units (such as geographical, product, functional) but complements them.

- Process organization supports standardization best.

- Process organization has limits set by customer relevance, output type, complexity of tasks, build-up of functional expertise and skill sets.

- Process organization is the most flexible organization type and the adequate answer to customer requirements in a constantly changing environment.

As organizing by processes seems to be the logical thing to do, it is often unclear what the difference between a typical functional organization and a process organization actually is. Is it just changing the AP department's name into PTP or team payables? The names play a big role but they are not sufficient to define it nor are they the core of it. The topic is not one of pure theoretical design nor is it about choosing one absolute alternative. Nevertheless, for understanding the differences, a polarized comparison is helpful. Let's have a look at a list of distinctive criteria in terms of process and functional organization, presented in Table 45.

Table 45 Process versus functional organization

	Process organization	Functional organization
Perspective of executives	Flexible groupings of interrelated work and information	Sets of discrete units with well-defined boundaries
Work orientation and output	Outward and customer-oriented	Upward and task-oriented
Purpose	Value creation Task performance	
Reporting	Mostly two reporting lines (shared/matrix)	One integrated reporting line (solid/dotted)
Measurement	Process goals	Unit goals
Compensation	Significant flexible part based on process performance	Fix (possibly with flexible unit-based bonus)
Employee selection	Based on process skills	Close scope specialists
Motivation	Work satisfaction	Advancement
Employee responsibility	Full-team responsibility for product/deliverable	Manager responsibility for performance of activity
Work assignment	Delivery-based	Activity-based
Work emphasis	Completing final product and delivering result	Completing individual task and compliance
Work order	Parallel	Sequential with integration points
Training target	Understanding of complex interrelations	Functional expertise
Career advancement	Personnel responsibility and/or task/scope increase and/or job rotation	Bottom to top levels with titles and personnel responsibility increase
Culture	Cooperative culture based on teamwork and entrepeneurship	Hierarchical culture-based upward fulfilment and error avoidance

continued

	Process organization	Functional organization
Executive skills	Coach with excellent operational knowledge and coordination skills	Manager with delegation and control skills
Management structures	Coexistence of different management structures	Single management structure
Management responsibility	End to end	Task/task group
People authority	Shared	Single
Technology alignment	Integrated workflow in line with supporting technology	Dispersed operations with technological interfaces
Organizational coverage	Supports virtual and network solutions	Can be aligned with competence centres (does not support virtual solutions)
Hierarchy levels	Few	Many
Control spans	High (20–50)	Low (5–20)
Change ability	High (high flexibility and knowledge dissemination)	Low (less innovation and siloed knowledge)
Maintenance requirements	High	Low

Most leaders of functional organizations get excited and angry about such a list as they feel their organization is being treated unfairly in this comparison, but it should only be a polarized exhibit of potential differences. Naturally it is difficult to implement a process organization because of a range of transformation hurdles, including:

- guarding and protecting old perspectives and privileges

- execution power remains in functional units

- two management structures working against each other and producing competency and responsibility fights

- lack of support of process organization by refusal to concede people and blocking of technical resources

- confusion produced by people pulling the matrix in two directions

- uncertainty of employees regarding orientation and career

- process improvements do not materialize.

Regardless of the implementation hurdles, it should become clear from the quite detailed client comparison example that process organization is an important topic to consider in the context of SSO, and the role of process organization can be summarized in ten points, as follows:

1. Process and functional orientations both have advantages and disadvantages and should coexist and must be balanced.

2. Customer-oriented processes and processes with high change ability have a stronger need to be process-oriented.

3. Simple transactional activities are mostly not 'value-adding' and need (additional) functional orientation.

4. Process orientation in SSO has often been used to support change aspects and partially reversed later.

5. Process organization is mainly a change in thinking.

6. Process view is also a question of scope view: processes too can accommodate functional specialist groups.

7. Process orientation must be supported by execution power.

8. Process orientation is necessary to support virtual solutions (a one-SSC solution could work on a stronger functional basis).

9. A possible final strategic goal of 'one SSC' or 'as few as possible lead administrations in SSO' is relevant for the standardization scope and hence for the necessity for process orientation.

10. Organizational change necessity is linked to magnitude of process change (streamlining, process innovation, process re-engineering).

To tackle the above issues and hurdles, some of the best practices that worked with other companies as general transformation support tools in changing to process organization include:

*   establishing consent for radical change in executive meetings
*   establishing process owners instead of (or in addition to) functional heads:
    – for project and as a permanent organizational solution
    – responsible for design, operations, measurement, training
    – acting as drivers for evolution
*   shifting organizational power, authority and budgets to the process owner:
    – budget by process instead of by department
    – link functional resources to process budgets

- measuring by process goals instead of unit goals, with linkage of performance and interests of both organization dimensions

- linking ratings, compensation and advancement to process-based KPI

- agreeing roles and responsibilities including decision-making (split) between functional and process units

- installing executive responsibility for the process implementation and operations

- agreeing together (between process owner and functional head) migration path to new organization

- installing escalation procedure and decision bodies to make decisions in case of disagreement (which will take place)

- finding a transfer solution for people who do not want to support new organization or dismissing them (based on three-tier people grouping)

- top management preventing negative communication to spread and increase opposition

- visibly relocating work to adjust working culture

- reconfiguring office space to support process team work

- involving complex communication and 'selling' of new organization using multiple channels and visible top-management support

- communicating cultural pillars and career perspectives answering individuals' concerns

- performing extensive training

- installing/enhancing business partnering (including business units)

- producing visible quick wins to support the change process.

Even though the process organization might be deemed 'a nice but unrealistic idea' by some, others have done it. It should be at least considered in the discussion about the future operating model and possibly it could be used as a target scenario, even if certain aspects of it cannot be reached (in the short term). An organization chart displaying the change from functional to process organization could look like the example in Figure 27, which is from a diversified consumer-goods company, where the move was made in connection with moving to eight sites in Phase One and one location targeted in Phase Two of the SSO project (CAO being used for 'chief administrative officer' – a 'reduced' CFO taking care of 'local' issues).

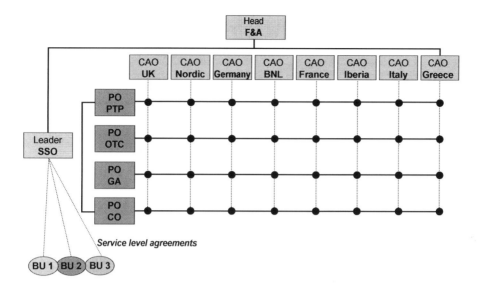

Figure 27   Organization: change to process orientation

The decision about when and how to make the change can be a difficult one. Often long discussions have to be completed to arrive at a decision – and not everybody wins. The overall organization has some key aspects to it:

- The process managers (links between functional and process view) are extremely important as they balance the traditional functional working views of the transaction teams and their desire for one clear reporting line with the 'two masters to please' in the matrix.

- Traditional CFOs are not needed at the point where power switches to the process view. Hence they need to get a different, reduced work scope (here CAO) or at least share the power.

- F&A heads will have to deal actively with escalation issues coming up from differences between functional and process view.

The detailed organization charts will naturally change too. An example for PTP, based on the above overall view, could look like Figure 28.

The real differences will be made visible when the target organization, organized by process orientation grouping similar activities and similar technologies, is compared to the current state. This has to be done on a very detailed level. In the beginning, all looks similar – in the end nothing stays where it was.

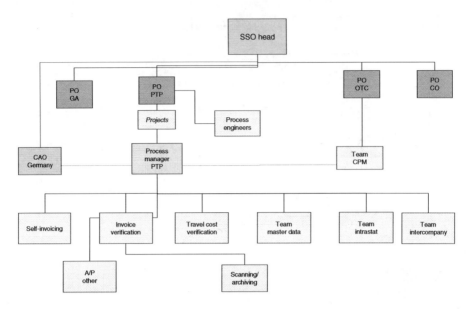

Figure 28   Process organization in PTP (example)

REMAINING LOCAL ORGANIZATION

One thing that is often forgotten in the SSO discussions is the fact that generally not all of the activities of any individual process are moved to the SSCs but some activities remain in the local units and, from an organizational point of view, these departments have to be reorganized. There is also an organizational activity to be performed on the remaining local organization.

A global automotive company, for example, had approximately 200 people engaged in the finance processes at one larger site. After the migration to the SSC, about 35–40 employees were left at the local site, 20% of the original workforce. Before, there were four large departments for the 200 employees. Obviously, it did not make any sense to keep the same number of departments as before. In fact, the number of departments will in most cases be reduced or even eliminated by attaching remaining activities to other departments. In this example, most people left at the local site were not the transactional clerks but the department heads and the group or team leaders. The problem with such a structure is that, apart from the organization chart issues, there is no reasonable hierarchy left as most remaining people are heads but have no employees to lead.

Fortunately for these people, there are also some new activities which will be introduced by the SSO. The remaining local finance people as well as the other functions have a new interface or link with the SSO which was not there before. This also involves change in the other functions. They need to get used to new persons who are possibly physically far away instead of at the end of the corridor. This new interface requires some work steps that are new:

- coordination between central and local units

- internal control of the new SSO (whether internal or external)

- measurement and control of the SSO as a supplier

- business partnering between all functions participating in a process.

This work can and should be defined in detail. In the above example, the claim-handling process produced the following detailed activities:

- Coordination:
    1. Claim type is unclear.
    2. Appropriate contact in local organization is not known.
    3. Resolution feedback from local organization is missing.
    4. Dealer addresses claim to local organization and SSC.

- Internal controls:
    1. Control if there are claim corrections without local instructions.
    2. Audit if SSC claim handling is corresponding with the instructions from local organization.
    3. Check if all claims are documented.

- Controlling/measurements:
    1. Number of claims per claim type.
    2. Average time to resolve a claim.
    3. Number and type of errors if claim is justified.

- Business partnering:
    1. Local departments involved: sales, pricing, marketing, logistics, dealer organization.
    2. Define general claim-handling responsibility.
    3. Create single-claim entry point (one face to the customer).
    4. Define claim reporting responsibility in local organization.

Of course, the documentation also includes detailed process flows with the exact placement of all these activities. Depending on the sum of these new activities, one can estimate the total workload in this field of relationship management and business partnering as shown in Figure 29.

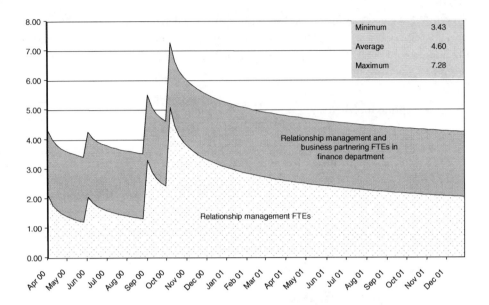

Minimum	3.43
Average	4.60
Maximum	7.28

Figure 29   New local tasks and new local organization required by an SSO

This overview exhibits the amount of new, additional FTEs required for the newly defined activities. All these FTEs are required locally. In the above example that would mean that, out of those 35 to 40 remaining employees, some three to eight FTEs (timing of need very project-specific) could be employed for these new tasks – 10 to 20% of the remaining headcount, in other words. These new activities are all more demanding work and suited for team leaders and those with similar skill sets.

The former department heads or finance heads have to run the relationship with the SSO as a relationship with a supplier, so there is a contract that needs to be enforced and reviewed. This is quite different from the direct management of people and therefore involves different activities. It is useful to look at all relationships between the SSC and the local units per level and separately for the project and for operations (see Figure 30).

The measurement piece of work should not be underestimated. In the beginning, a benchmarking or measurement team might make sense. Workload will be substantial in the beginning, but will diminish over time (in terms of resources required). Possibly the measurement team then will be one person integrated into another team.

Overall, the local organization changes dramatically, not only because of activities moved away to an SSC, but because of different types of changes:

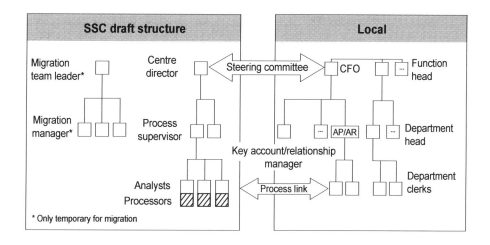

Figure 30   Organizational set-up of links between local organization and SSC

- original activities remaining local but with need of organizational restructuring

- new activities because of the SSC in areas of (SSC) relationship management and business partnering.

Areas to be considered when redesigning the local organization include:

Structure:
- number of layers
- spans of control
- working structure (process, functional, country teams)
- reporting responsibilities.

Decision-making:
- approval levels
- decision-making authority within the structure
- internal controls check.

Tasks:
- tasks in scope
- tasks out of scope
- new tasks
- role set-up.

People:
- basic skills and abilities
- skill delta and skill development
- training plan and set-up.

Information:
- information and document flow
- supporting IT structure.

Rewards:
- employee motivation and rewards.

BUSINESS PARTNERING

Many people discuss business partnering and so did we under the local organization topic above. Unfortunately it seems to be something hard to get a grip on in terms of exact definitions. Here is some help to define business partnering:

What is BUSINESS PARTNERING?

Business partnering is a strategic role that builds relationships between finance and the businesses. Business partners will provide in-depth financial analysis and expertise to assist decision-making within company departments. Business partners act as links between functions. Hence, business partnering is a term used to describe the value-adding role of finance to the business.

This vision for finance (of being a business partner) can and should be further refined through a real company initiative to determine how finance could support the business better. During such an initiative, one example company interviewed the managers of the different business units about what they would want from a business partner. It was found that business-unit managers wanted a business partner:

- to 'live and breathe my business'
- to be proactive in identifying problems and giving solutions, not just figures
- to be able to say 'no' to my management team
- not to block deals but to provide better solutions
- to understand the commercial implications of decisions.

In the smaller countries, the business partner could be the finance director. In larger countries, there will be several business partners, sometimes even dedicated to one business unit alone. The managing director and country management team should identify the exact number of business partners required for their country.

A detailed job description for the business partner role is necessary to outline the key responsibilities of this position. General competencies identified as being important for a business partner and to be reviewed when defining the role include:

- interpersonal skills (includes networking, influencing, managing conflict)
- technical skills (includes accounting expertise, knowledge of current accounting thinking)

- business skills (includes strategic thinking, market knowledge, business acumen)

- personal skills (includes confidence, commitment to results)

- mental aptitude (includes analytical ability and accuracy).

Clearly, this represents a change in the way many finance departments are supporting the business today. That change will vary depending on the business needs of each subsidiary (a small growing subsidiary may have different analytical needs than a larger, more stable subsidiary) and what people and skills they currently have in their organization.

The way to achieve the business partnering aspect of the vision for finance will depend on each company's and each country entity's specific circumstances and the specific skills and experiences of the individual business partners. To facilitate this evolution, the following process has proven successful:

- *Review business-partner job description:* when individuals are selected for the function of business partner, they should receive the job description for their role as well as information on skills and competencies.

- *Discuss expectations with relevant business units:* the first action they should take is to set up a meeting with the BU head(s) they support to discuss customer expectations and explore the added value they can bring to the BU.

- *Attend business-partner induction:* within the first six months of their assignment, they should attend a business-partner induction course. This course explores the skills and competencies needed for the function and provides tools for incumbents to assess their own capabilities. The result of this should be a personal development plan, followed by recommended training courses that the business partners can take in their home country or which are offered centrally by internal training.

- *Establish coaching structure:* it is recommended that each induction class has a coach, assigned by the F&A community, who will bring the class together in the future so that they can share knowledge and learning. This coach should be a senior F&A leader, who has experience in business partnering and who can act as an advisor to the group.

Business partnering is a role that is critical in setting up an SSO since almost all finance work will follow processes that cross functional borders and in addition move between central and local sites. There will be a range of different business partnering roles both between the SSO and remaining local finance as well as between finance and other functions.

GOVERNANCE

Especially in North America, the governance model has become a major component of the SSO. Naturally the issues around it are relevant for everybody but the discussion around the governance topic seems to excite Americans more than others. In Europe, the governance issues are often summarized under organization issues, hence the placing of the topic here in this chapter.

Governance is described differently, but in essence it is about the necessity to organize and guide the different constituents of an SSO. As Figure 31 shows, the constituencies of a shared services organization are wide and dispersed. They include customers (such as business units, corporate, company employees, banks), information providers (vendors, company employees), stakeholders (company management, BU management) and influencers (corporate audit). These groups have a vested interest in the success (or failure) of the SSO and should be used to help the centre(s) on the road to success.

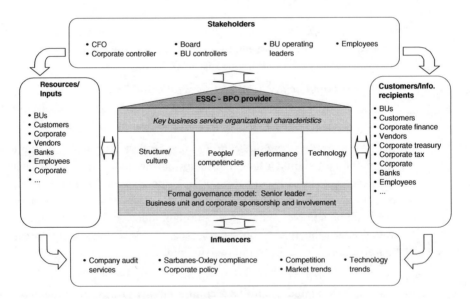

Figure 31   The constituents of the SSO

The governance model is necessary to successfully manage these constituents and their relationships to each other. Involving representatives from these constituency groups in a well-defined shared services governance model is required to successfully operate the centre and manage any outsource relationships that may be 'housed' within the overall shared services structure. Based on a US example, the governance model was described as follows:

- A well-defined governance model provides direction and focus to ensure that the SSO or BPO provider continually strives towards world-class performance.

- The governance model must include the 'voice of the customer' to ensure that the services delivered are those required and to provide their support to the improvement process.

- The governance model helps to resolve conflicts by providing a defined structure and process for issue resolution.

- This model includes clear and communicated roles and responsibilities.

The governance model, hence, is a combination of strategy, management and organization issues focusing on:

- roles and responsibilities

- reporting lines

- escalation procedures.

It also complements the organization design.

Best practices in governance show that the governance model in general consists of the following components:

- *Executive board:* consists of an executive-level decision-making group that sets performance targets and annual operating plans; approves capital expenditures; agrees to scope changes.

- *Customer council:* consists of mid-management and focuses their efforts on identifying 'end-to-end process' improvement opportunities, provides advice on prioritization and seconds resources to participate in the solution development and deployment to ensure success.

- *SSO or BPO provider strategic leadership:* is responsible for the operation of the centre.

- *Process leaders:* are responsible for the day-to-day operation of the process teams within the SSC.

An example of a possible set-up is presented in Figure 32. The multi-layered governance model depicted in Figure 32 is critical as it allows each group to focus on what they can control and act on. Each individual level cannot act on its own:

- Executive board level can make the critical financial and other decisions impacting the overall company but they cannot spend time on the details of the SSO to understand the top issues.

- The customer council can set the appropriate targets of performance for the SSO but often cannot make the capital and operating budget decisions required.

- Shared service leadership can operate the day-to-day aspects of the centre but cannot rally the required attention and priority of the business to enact change on its own.

The amount of levels and parties included can vary. The governance model also must state clearly time intervals for meetings inside the structure and decision-making rules and time lines. Escalation procedures should be designed in detail, with every level defined, clear decision points, time definitions (such as how many days to solve an issue) and how the process runs.

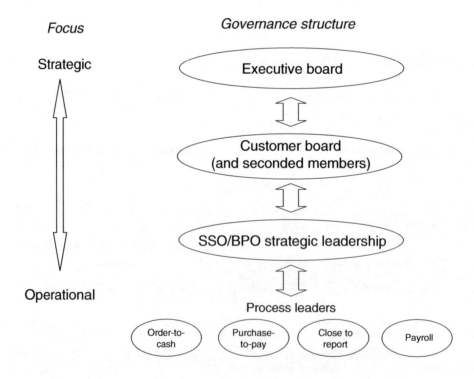

Figure 32   Example governance model

PART II

Implementing Shared Services

Someone once said: 'Just to change will not guarantee it will be better, but to be better we will have to change.' There are a lot of fears out there of shared services – some of them, for sure, are worthwhile having. Nevertheless, shared services is just a methodology, maybe just a tool, to reach the constant improvement targets by which our society is driven. We need to become better, always. Hence it is necessary to be proactive and use all tools available before they are being used on you.

Part II will deal with implementing shared services. It complements Part I, which described the topic and detailed aspects in terms of general understanding and possible target vision. In Part II the target audience is mainly those individuals who 'need actually to do it': implement shared services, run a project and run the SSO. We will base our approach and the structure of Part II of this book on our five-phase methodology that has proven to be almost as good as a natural law. Even when deviated from, it provides an indispensable checklist for any project manager or CFO.

FIVE-PHASE-IMPLEMENTATION METHODOLOGY

All shared service projects and operations follow a similar lifecycle. All projects have similar topics to discuss and issues to solve. The content of the SSO projects can be structured in different ways, but the structure proven to us to be the most useful is the five-phase-SSO approach (see Figure 33).

In the following chapters we will deal with the content of each phase in detail.

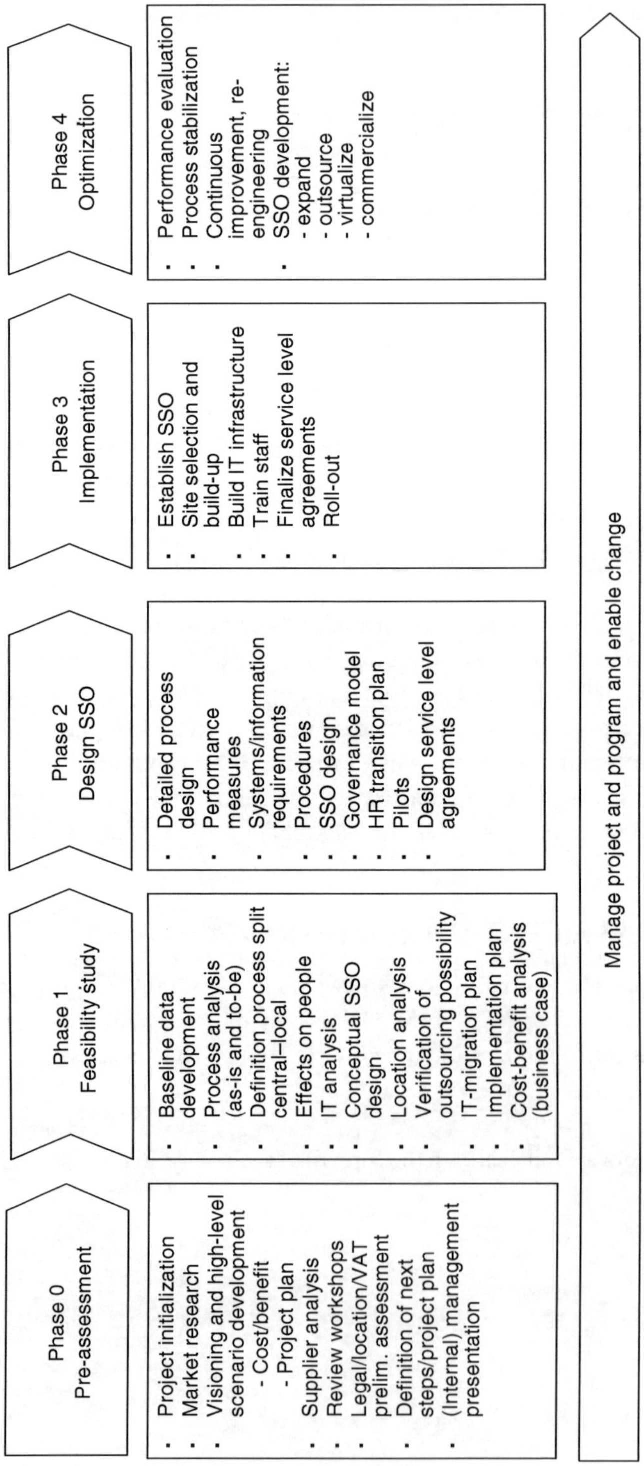

Phase 0 Pre-assessment	Phase 1 Feasibility study	Phase 2 Design SSO	Phase 3 Implementation	Phase 4 Optimization
· Project initialization · Market research · Visioning and high-level scenario development - Cost/benefit - Project plan · Supplier analysis · Review workshops · Legal/location/VAT prelim. assessment · Definition of next steps/project plan · (Internal) management presentation	· Baseline data development · Process analysis (as-is and to-be) · Definition process split central–local · Effects on people · IT analysis · Conceptual SSO design · Location analysis · Verification of outsourcing possibility · IT-migration plan · Implementation plan · Cost-benefit analysis (business case)	· Detailed process design · Performance measures · Systems/information requirements · Procedures · SSO design · Governance model · HR transition plan · Pilots · Design service level agreements	· Establish SSO · Site selection and build-up · Build IT infrastructure · Train staff · Finalize service level agreements · Roll-out	· Performance evaluation · Process stabilization · Continuous improvement, re-engineering · SSO development: - expand - outsource - virtualize - commercialize

Manage project and program and enable change

Figure 33   Five-phase shared service organization approach

CHAPTER 9

Pre-Assessment

PROJECT INITIALIZATION OF PHASE ZERO

We call the first phase 'Phase Zero' instead of 'Phase One', because these pre-assessment activities are performed mostly before there is a budget and an official project. The pre-assessment activities start with someone hearing about shared services and trying to find out more about it. This could be a piece of information picked up from a competitor, a conference, or book or article. Vendors or customers could point out that a solution called shared services exists and should be explored. Anyone reading this book has gone through this step already – possibly also having received the task to look at SSOs by someone who picked up the topic somewhere else.

MARKET RESEARCH

After some initial investigation there will be a desire or a need to look at SSOs in terms of collecting information about them. Information about SSOs can be collected by different means including:

- *Literature*: reading books such as this one. There are surprisingly few books on the topic and most are very theoretical, but literature is a comprehensive information source. In addition there are articles on SSOs in daily papers as well as in business and finance magazines. There are also dedicated SSO publications, such as *Shared Service News*.

- *Conferences*: there are numerous SSO conferences. You can find one every month somewhere and for sure every year at least once near you. There are at least five conference companies with serious offerings on SSOs including IQPC (Shared Services and Outsourcing Network), Ark Group (Shared Service Practitioner), IIR, Marcus Evans, Management Circle and some others to choose from. Visiting a conference is a very useful way to get an overview of what other companies have done.

- *Collaborative learning*: having understood what SSO is about, the next steps are often the search for ways to implement it and the fight to convince yourself and others that it can work. Here, information exchange with other companies is very helpful. You can do this on a bilateral basis which is good, but the more professional way is to use ready-made collaborative platforms, for example The Hackett Group's Business Advisory Services, to meet others with the same interest.

- *External advisory:* another useful way is to have consultants explain what can be done. This gives you a better overview on the alternatives and can speed up the process significantly.

The market research is an information-collection activity and it lasts as long as it takes for the performer to gain the subjective feeling of having enough information. This can be very different from company to company. Some companies go through this information gathering in some weeks; others are known to have performed extensive site visits over 12–18 months, discussing with up to 20 other companies and evaluating the idea. In our experience, the pre-assessment should not take more than three or four months as you will otherwise lose the momentum.

VISIONING AND HIGH-LEVEL SCENARIO DEVELOPMENT

The distinction between activities performed in Phase Zero and Phase One is not always 100% clear. Some activities need to be performed twice but using different levels of detail. One such task is the scenario development. It is something actually performed in detail in the feasibility study (Phase One), but it is useful and often necessary to have at least a basic understanding of potential scenarios before a feasibility study can start. This thought process is also necessary to be able to define the feasibility scope better.

Several companies perform something like a high-level feasibility study. This basically involves the activities of the feasibility study but with less detail, less time, fewer resources and lower cost. This high-level approach is often performed partly or fully inside the pre-assessment phase, without an official and specified SSO project budget. In some cases it is possible to leave out detailed components of the assessment. This is mainly dependent on how convinced a company is about an SSO being the correct solution. Three examples are:

1. Based on significant pre-assessment work, a pharmaceutical company performed a three-month feasibility study globally paying a seven-digit number just on external help.

2. A manufacturing company performed a high-level feasibility study inside the pre-assessment phase totalling three weeks with a five-digit external invoice.

3. A retail company performed two workshops with external help and completed the remaining work based on the guidelines with some internal resources inside a total time window of two months.

All the above examples are large companies (between €3 and €15 billion in sales). In cases 1 and 3 a design phase followed; in case 2 the idea was abolished. This should demonstrate that the pre-assessment and attached feasibility work can have very different levels of detail and still be successful or not successful. We feel that, in case 2, a detailed approach would have been necessary due to the strong internal resistance to the project. A three-week high-level assessment did deliver the relevant information but the detailed questions of reluctant parts of management could not always be answered. This can lead to loss of credibility, even though the case might be strong, just because certain aspects are not covered.

Whether the pre-assessment scenario piece is pre-work or is supposed to cover the feasibility activities in full, it is a necessary work piece that can be started by thinking about the strategic options in general. For this purpose, a visioning session based on the strategic options map approach is useful (see Figure 34).

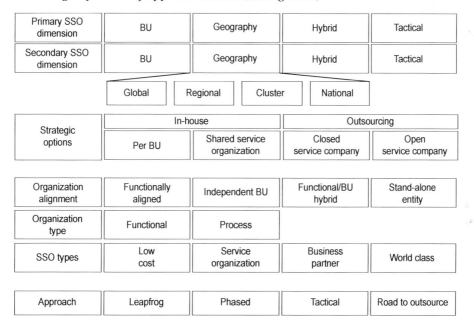

Figure 34   The SSO strategic options map

This session should be prepared based on market research and carried out with the CFO and then other finance managers should be selected to evaluate the thoughts behind it. It is useful to link the targets to the alternative approaches and try to get a more detailed understanding of the 'SSO strategy'. It is not advisable to spread the pre-assessment work onto too many persons; neither is it advisable, even in open environments, to start broad discussions at this point.

In most cases the first issue in large companies is to decide between scoping dimensions: do you want to consolidate by geography or by business unit? Often differing views exist. It is useful to find out whether the target view is one about a 'world-class' organization or 'low cost', 'best practice', 'business partnering' and so on, as such simplified terms give valuable hints as to the strategic intent.

One result of the visioning exercise should be a vision statement accompanied by goals and relevant components to consider. One consumer-goods company came up with: 'Deliver highest level of compliance and productivity aligned with business objectives' as the vision and broke that down into the goals:

1. Lowest risk with lower cost, and

2. Lowest cost.

The vision components to look at were defined as:

● deliver value to business

● be fully compliant

● be efficient/low cost

● deliver in a sustainable way.

These results can look different for different companies. The important thing is to go through the activity and just do it. This is faster than discussing the necessity.

The high-level scenarios are mainly about:

● Should we go for SSO or also think about external outsourcing?

● What is our geographical and business scope?

● What would some alternatives look like in terms of approach?

These and similar questions need to be answered internally before a serious feasibility study can even be scoped. The thinking could be done based on the matrix shown in Figure 35. It could result in a preliminary, high-level view on what work could be done in what way, as in Figure 36.

The high-level scenario development can also include a rough estimate on the potential financial investment and benefits. Such a business case developed in the pre-assessment can never be down to the last detail, but if the company has a reasonable amount of data available centrally, the high-level estimates from the pre-assessment can be accurate enough to base the first decisions on. On such a high level, there could be four main alternative scenarios:

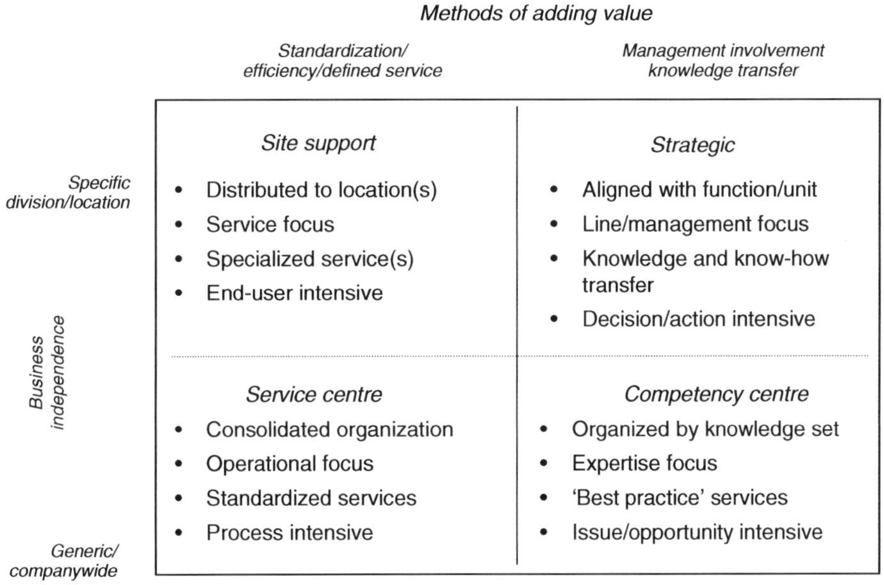

Methods of adding value

Standardization/
efficiency/defined service

Management involvement
knowledge transfer

Specific
division/location

Site support

- Distributed to location(s)
- Service focus
- Specialized service(s)
- End-user intensive

Strategic

- Aligned with function/unit
- Line/management focus
- Knowledge and know-how transfer
- Decision/action intensive

Business
independence

Service centre

- Consolidated organization
- Operational focus
- Standardized services
- Process intensive

Competency centre

- Organized by knowledge set
- Expertise focus
- 'Best practice' services
- Issue/opportunity intensive

Generic/
companywide

Figure 35   A conceptual view of shared services

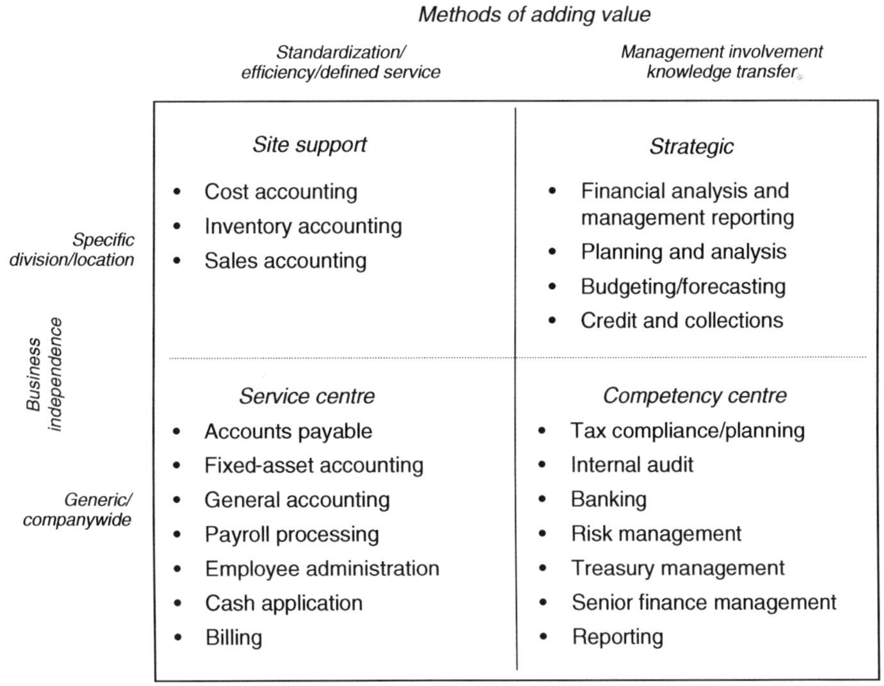

Methods of adding value

Standardization/
efficiency/defined service

Management involvement
knowledge transfer

Site support

- Cost accounting
- Inventory accounting
- Sales accounting

Strategic

- Financial analysis and management reporting
- Planning and analysis
- Budgeting/forecasting
- Credit and collections

Specific
division/location

Business
independence

Service centre

- Accounts payable
- Fixed-asset accounting
- General accounting
- Payroll processing
- Employee administration
- Cash application
- Billing

Competency centre

- Tax compliance/planning
- Internal audit
- Banking
- Risk management
- Treasury management
- Senior finance management
- Reporting

Generic/
companywide

Figure 36   Financial processes in shared services

- outsourcing

- shared services with full scope

- regional clusters in shared services

- local re-engineering (without SSO).

The results would be estimated ranges of financial benefits and costs, perhaps 5–10% savings in the local re-engineering scenario and 25–35% savings in the SSO case. The supporting materials cannot be complete and a range of assumptions will still need to be evaluated and confirmed.

SUPPLIER ANALYSIS

The views about using external help vary from company to company, so every company will make their own decision about selecting a consultant or some other external supplier. In general, it is advisable to go by logic and benefit, not by principle. As an example, a consumer-goods company set up their key success factors for the project and then evaluated whether these could be fulfilled better with external help:

- Value proposition:
    - business case as economic justification
    - accountability of results.

- Sense of urgency:
    - results-driven approach
    - quick wins to produce self-funding change programme.

- Management support:
    - leadership commitment
    - cross-functional and cross-BU involvement of senior management.

- Best practices:
    - common/best/better practice implementation
    - integrated business solutions combining people, processes and technology.

- Change and knowledge transfer:
    - effective management of people and cultural issues
    - built-in transfer of knowledge in the organization.

- Performance measurement:
    - monitor and sustain effectiveness of change initiative.

Based on this list, the potential benefits from an external consultant and hence the reasons to use a consultant were summarized in four categories:

- *Expertise acquisition*: avoid mistakes made by other companies.

- *Results-driven orientation*: structured and disciplined approach to bridge functional and technological silos; neutral position of a consultant.

- *Knowledge transfer*: integrated and interactive approach enhances organizational learning.

- *Resource leverage*: use of consultants increases flexibility and enables better utilization of human resources.

The result of the evaluation was: all aspects considered, the project carried out with consultant support is cheaper. The consumer-goods company then engaged external help.

Using external advisors is not a black-and-white decision. Often successful solutions are somewhere in the middle, for instance:

- use consultants for those parts that they are good at and do the rest internally – do not outsource the project and then complain about lost knowledge;

- do not invent the wheel again on everything 'just because you can' – even for fast and clever people 'double work is double work'.

Other suppliers of know-how relevant to an SSO project might be:

- collaborative learning programmes and their advisors, for example The Hackett Group

- investment agencies of selected countries for location information

- HR consultancies for market information and people selection

- training companies for training missing skill sets and enabling change

- Six Sigma trainers and other improvement programme sources

- conference companies for contact information and information on newest developments

- providers of technical solutions for certain processes, for example IT software providers.

Most of these suppliers cannot be chosen immediately because the need for them is not clear in the pre-assessment. One or two trusted advisors should be enough to start with. The relevant decision points for support are once for the feasibility phase and then again for design and implementation.

PRELIMINARY LOCATION, LEGAL AND REGULATORY REVIEW

The detailed analysis on legal and regulatory issues will be carried out in the feasibility study. In the pre-assessment it makes sense to supplement the high-level scenario analysis with a preliminary longlist on locations. These can also be checked broadly against potential show stoppers from a legal and regulatory point of view. This assessment can be done by pulling together externally available studies and selected external support in the form of workshops. A detailed legal analysis about, for instance, the options to set up legal entities with different ownership structures is not an activity for the pre-assessment.

PROJECT PLAN

The pre-assessment activities should come up with a result including a project plan. The focus here should be on the next one to two phases, especially on whether to invest money into a feasibility phase. A project plan is tied to resources performing the project and the search for internal resources should be started; it has proven helpful to be able to present names in a final presentation. The project timing should be clear in terms of start and approximate length in months or years. It is not necessary to have all milestones and steering committee meetings fixed. This will happen in Phase One.

INTERNAL MANAGEMENT PRESENTATION

Typically the pre-assessment starts with the request from the CFO or head of finance to review the topic of shared services and ends with an internal management presentation on the outcome of this information collection and assessment exercise. This internal presentation will need to be prepared with care, especially if the goal is to support and 'sell' the idea of building an SSO. The result of the presentation will need to be:

- a decision on pursuing the idea further
- (in case the idea is estimated to be potentially beneficial) a project with resources and a budget installed
- a first project plan draft and next steps agreed upon
- a draft project structure including key players such as the project manager, as well as members of the steering committee
- a general decision made on open or 'hidden' feasibility study.

In our experience, the ability to recommend the openness of such project activities depends largely on the company culture. However, the ground rule should be to try to communicate as much as possible. The openness will open doors, even when decisions are difficult, and most things will be carried through the company by rumours anyway, so it is often better to manage them actively.

CHAPTER 10

The Feasibility Study and Business Case

THE NECESSITY FOR THE FEASIBILITY STUDY

The feasibility study, sometimes also called an opportunity assessment, is the first large and quite clearly defined piece of work to be done on the way to shared services. The feasibility study is actually not the same as a business case, which is the product of the feasibility study, but the terminology is used in such a way that a business case could also refer to the whole work of producing a business case and would then be equal to this whole phase. Interestingly, the feasibility study terminology is used more in Europe, where concentration obviously is on the purpose and content of the work. In North America companies tend to speak about the business case focusing more on the outcome and results of the work.

A feasibility phase is not defined legally or in any other way as mandatory, but practically all the work inside the feasibility study has to be done anyway to be successful, so in almost 100% of cases the feasibility study takes place (under whatever name). Also, this workload is too big to be performed as a side exercise without a real project budget. Our SSO database with detailed data on approximately 800 SSOs tells us that, out of all these companies, merely one claims to have been successful in implementing their SSO without top-management support and a project budget in this phase.

BASELINE DATA AND BENCHMARKING

The feasibility study has two main areas of interest, the quantitative baseline data and the qualitative evaluation of these data. Practically, there is no way around the measurement of the baseline data. The baseline will be necessary in the start-up phase of the SSO as well as in the operations later. The baseline data are necessary for such reasons as:

- providing quantitative information about status quo (where are we today – are we good or bad?)

- providing financial input to business case (what is our cost and performance position and how big is the opportunity for the future?)

- providing target data in future to measure against (did we meet the objectives of the business case?)

- providing a measurement system baseline (what do we need to achieve and break down in scorecards and against what are variable bonuses paid, and so on?)

- providing a steering system baseline (how do we set KPIs and build SLAs and what best practices do we need?).

Hardly any company has baseline data available, that is, data about their finance cost by process and including full process cost, not just the cost inside the finance function. Also, performance data – data on performance of companies, teams and individuals, such as cost per invoice, invoices booked per year, cycle times, closing times, response times and error rates – are not always available. Sometimes individual data cannot be available due to data security reasons: in several European countries the measurement of individual performance can be legally restricted.

The best way to produce the baseline is to benchmark. Bottom-up measuring methods are so complicated and costly and benchmarking has proven to be so accurate that it does not make sense to consider any other methods. In benchmarking, different views are possible:

- external benchmark
  - overall
  - inside industry
  - for defined geography
  - for specific peer group, for example with same complexity

- internal benchmark

- benchmarking over time.

Benchmarking results can be looked upon at a specific point in time as well as over time; for example, a comparison of a company's cost of finance as a percentage of revenue from one year to another. Years ago companies preferred industry benchmarks or national benchmarks. Today it is accepted that such a scope limitation also limits the outcome and is not beneficial. However, benchmarking should be on the 'apples-to-apples' basis, so it is necessary to consider some ground rules in selecting a benchmarking provider:

- Consider only process-orientated benchmarking that evaluates efficiency and effectiveness at process level, as an SSO is a process-oriented project.

- 'Apples-to-apples' requires significant database and clear complexity definitions.

- A strong comparability of the results based on strict and longstanding definitions of processes and metrics is necessary.

- Flexibility to provide industry and country data in addition to overall data is useful.

- Data must be 'actual' data – The Hackett Group throws comparison data older than two years out of the comparison database.

- Available database must be of significant size to be sure of 'statistical truth'.

- The pure data are useless – they must be accompanied by best-practices information and next-steps advice.

- The benchmarking exercise should not be a project of its own with significant cost and time required, but instead should be an easy exercise with little money and resources needed – methodology, tools and support provided are key.

- A process that ensures the quality of data input and also results in a proper database for comparison is essential.

- In the analysis the comparison must consider the demand drivers and structural factors of your organization.

Based on these rules and criteria, some key points to consider in benchmarking include that it needs to be comprehensive in terms of scope of measurement; it must include all relevant cost and performance factors comprising people, technology, process and information (see Figure 37).

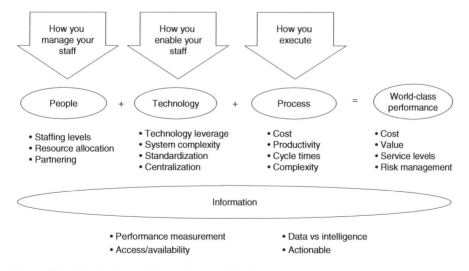

Figure 37   Key business drivers in a world-class company

A measurement of process efficiency alone is useless as is the measurement of technology alone. The 'big picture' consists of putting together the puzzle made of all the individual pieces: a range of measurements. The drivers behind the results must be identified and considered; they must be both structural and demand drivers (see Figure 38).

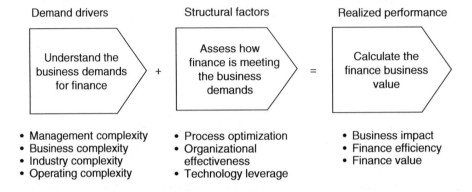

Demand drivers

> Understand the business demands for finance

- Management complexity
- Business complexity
- Industry complexity
- Operating complexity

\+

Structural factors

> Assess how finance is meeting the business demands

- Process optimization
- Organizational effectiveness
- Technology leverage

\=

Realized performance

> Calculate the finance business value

- Business impact
- Finance efficiency
- Finance value

Figure 38   Drivers and factors influencing performance

Demand drivers, exhibiting the environment in which the company operates, may comprise:

- products
- customers
- suppliers
- geographies
- employees
- business organization structure
- competitive environment
- regulatory environment
- rate of business change
- capital structure.

Structural factors of the business may include:

- strategic alignment
- process complexity

- policy governance

- application complexity

- sourcing strategy

- organization structure

- staffing levels

- skills

- analytical tools.

The realized performance as a result of the demand drivers and structural factors is based on:

- ROI

- cost of service

- business impact

- operating efficiency

- technology leverage

- labour costs

- accuracy of information

- cycle time

- reliability of forecasts.

The benchmarking results must be measured not only based on efficiency but also value, as shown in Figure 39.

Such a review typically, based on The Hackett Group as an example, includes value and efficiency content for each of the five dimensions:

- Strategic alignment
  - comprehensiveness of finance vision
  - linkage to business plan.

- Partnering
  - linkage to operations
  - collaboration with suppliers and customers.

- Organization
  - spans of control

- process fragmentation
- decision-support ratios
- people development.

- Technology
  - complexity, internal integration
  - innovation and information access.

- Process
  - productivity, unit cost
  - service and quality.

For the feasibility study, and to complete the business case, one needs initially the internal as-is baseline data and the external benchmarking data, because only the external comparison will allow one to quantify the potential improvement gap. Later, in operations, the benchmarks are useful again. In summary, the necessity of benchmarking in the context with SSO includes the following reasons and uses:

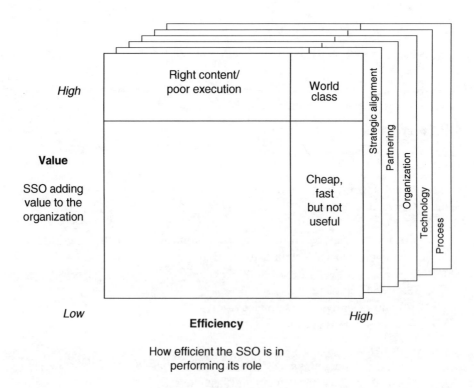

Figure 39   Five dimensions for value and efficiency in measurement of performance

- Establishing a baseline for current finance shared services.

- Comparing performance across industries.

- Rapidly distinguishing between non-value-added finance activities and those resources essential to future growth.

- Identifying key drivers of the finance-SSO performance.

- Getting best-practices insight and learning from others.

- Prioritizing short- and long-term opportunities.

- Defining tangible benefits and next steps.

The benchmarking itself needs to be tightly linked to the other work packages inside the feasibility study. Hence the process descriptions, for example, should be identical. Because the external benchmarking definitions cannot be changed for the purpose of one project, it is useful to take over the definitions from a benchmark provider and use them also for the process review and later the design. Possibly some small differences must be considered and additional processes included in the benchmarking or in the process review.

A good benchmarking also delivers reasons for the measured performance, for instance a list of best practices and their internal utilization compared with external utilization of the same best practices. Best practices is synonymous with a well-managed business and can be looked upon by basically the same dimensions as the benchmarking itself, value and efficiency. Best practices provide a benefit because they are proven to help companies:

- drive top decile (top 10%) efficiency and value

- leverage proven technology

- enhance quality, cost and speed

- ensure effective control

    They simply work!

Common practices that only drive one of the two dimensions, value or efficiency, should not be considered best practices, as they will result in either the right content but poor execution, or cheap and fast but not useful results. Only coverage of both dimensions can produce best practices.

Some distinguish between practices, better common practices and best practices; some use all these terms for the same topic. Some companies also use the terminology

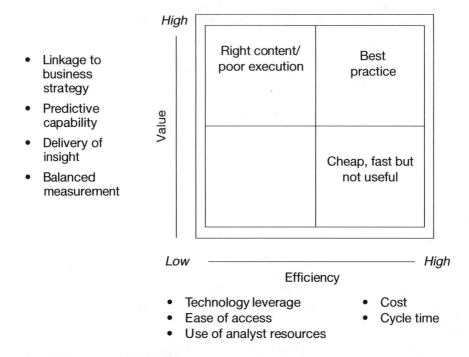

- Linkage to business strategy
- Predictive capability
- Delivery of insight
- Balanced measurement

- Technology leverage
- Ease of access
- Use of analyst resources

- Cost
- Cycle time

Figure 40   Best-practice definition

in the way that best practices are externally valid working ways, whereas the ones that are applicable to oneself are 'best-fitting practices'. The terminology does not matter, as long as it is clear that the target is to 'steal good ideas from others' and not re-invent the wheel, and that this can only be achieved by looking at what others are doing and how successful they are in doing so. Questions around best practices that should be answered during this phase are:

- Identification of the best practice:
  - What performance drives this best practice?
  - Is it a common best practice or is it depending on specific conditions?
  - Is it a new best practice or does it get replaced soon?

- Understanding of the best practice:
  - What does the best practice mean in detail?
  - What works and what does not work in the implementation?
  - What is the business base?

The one point often missed is the life expectancy of the best practice. Some good ideas are used by almost everyone today, but we all agree that new technology will replace them in the future. Hence, the fact that a majority is doing something is not sufficient to prove it is good nor that it will last. As an example we mentioned earlier that 50% of companies use workflow and imaging in PTP and OTC. This has proven to be a very successful tool and definitely is a best practice, even if only half of the companies use it. On the other hand, outsourcing the mail room including all scanning and even the pre-sorting and OCR could be the solution preferred tomorrow; alternatively it could be the digitalization solutions such as OB10.

BUSINESS-MODEL REVIEW

Before the analysis work begins, it is advisable to perform a business-model review. This is advisable also for internal project members, as the overall business model of a group could well be carried out very differently in different geographies. Such a review should include:

- how business is done, in other words what business model is used (trading, manufacturing and so on)

- who are the customers and what are their requirements

- what framework is the business working in (free economy, regulated environment)

- what are the business requirements to the support processes, for instance finance

- what legal structures are used.

At the end of such a review, which can take some days or some weeks depending on scope, all project members will have a better understanding of the company's business and how it is being performed. This common understanding helps agreement on terminology to be used and enables the process analysis to be completed faster.

Process analysis (as-is and to-be)

The process analysis is one of the key activities inside the feasibility study. Together with the benchmarking, these two work pieces are the foundation on which all other work will be built.

The process analysis itself has two parts:

- *As-is analysis:* the analysis of the processes in their current state.

- *To-be analysis:* the brainstorming about the future process design.

As-is analysis

The target of the as-is analysis is to review the processes in their current state and understand how the processes are carried out in different entities and geographies and why this is the case. On the basis of the business-model review and the defined project scope, processes are first selected and sorted. It is useful to stick to the same process definitions used in the benchmarking. In any case, standard definitions are necessary and, to be successful, must be adhered to very strictly. There will always be certain processes in certain countries or entities where the standard process model does not fit perfectly. The model should not be changed though: the differences should be documented. If the model really does not work, then it must be changed, but for everybody. This can be done more easily at the beginning of the project. Later on, this will result in massive rework. In general it can be stated that:

- standard process models in existence and provided by benchmarking or consulting companies do the work and need very little changes;
- based on a process model (with a list and possibly numbering of processes) the company needs to define the list of sub-processes relevant for the project.

The definition of the final sub-process list will take days, sometimes weeks. It is well-invested time, though, as any mistakes here will be very hard to correct later. Based on a standard process model, one consumer-goods company developed the following initial sub-process list for PTP:

- PTP Process 01: Invoice verification with reference to a purchase order (PO).
- PTP Process 02: Self-invoicing/evaluated receipt settlement (ERS).
- PTP Process 03: Invoice verification without reference to a purchase order.
- PTP Process 04: Credit memo/debit memo handling.
- PTP Process 05: Goods received/invoice received maintenance.
- PTP Process 06: Invoice verification for incoming freights.
- PTP Process 07: Intrastat reporting.
- PTP Process 08: Electronic processed invoice verification with PO.
- PTP Process 09: Vendor account reconciliation.
- PTP Process 10: Down payments.
- PTP Process 11: Vendor claim handling.
- PTP Process 12: Vendor dunning.
- Reporting and statistics.

This list was changed somewhat during the coming months and at the end of the project had 16 processes.

Using the process model and the sub-process list, the process teams can start their work and review the processes. This activity can be done in several different ways, but should include:

- collecting and reading available process materials (for example past projects);
- review team internal discussion of the processes;
- site visits to validate understanding of process work and resources applied;
- documentation of processes;
- validation of documentation and understanding with local sites.

In the as-is process review, the reading and discussing of existing process materials is often not that useful because most of the materials are outdated and processes have possibly changed since that documentation was done. Relatively new process documentation is useful as a basis, but the relevant information can only be gathered at the local sites. Therefore the process teams must visit the sites in scope to discuss the processes. To save cost and time, a selection of sites to be visited can be carried out. Criteria for the selection could include some or all of the following:

- different businesses included
- different IT platforms included
- large and small units included
- known process differences included
- political reasons.

Based on the criteria and the available timing, a selection should be made to be as small as possible but as big as necessary. The 80–20 rule works fine here too but, in addition, it is wise to think about potentially problematic sites and include them on the list for 'political reasons'.

The site visits are a politically difficult task. The local employees will feel frightened about this visit and hence these visits need significant preparation from management in terms of communication. It has proven useful and necessary to carry out these visits. Some companies have tried to perform this work as a 'secret back-office exercise' only. This cannot realistically work – the results can only be as detailed as the work in the pre-assessment, no more. The risk in the decision-making is so big that most decisions then will be against implementing. If communicated correctly, the site visits will be successful in terms of local cooperation and getting the necessary information to build the business case. The actual process review activity is delicate and the staffing of this activity should consider the project risk associated with inexperienced people performing it.

An important part of the site visits inside the as-is analysis is the FTE collection per sub-process and activity. It might seem strange to do this, because many expect the benchmarking to have delivered this data already. The answer is: benchmarking will never deliver this detail – if it did, it would not be benchmarking but process analysis. This FTE collection will also validate the benchmarking results and give all project members and affected parties more trust in the quantitative basis of the business case. The relevant question here is often: should the benchmarking be carried out before or after the site visits? We recommend doing the benchmarking first and then build on those results when performing the site visits. The big benefit is that the process teams will have preliminary knowledge about the benchmarking results when they travel to the sites. This outweighs the need for possible double work by the local employees and their view that things are being done twice and hence are uncoordinated.

The information necessary cannot be collected from all sites by physical visits because of time and resource constraints. Therefore some of the sites and their information must be collected by questionnaires or other means of non-physical data collection. These data need to be included in the overall results. In terms of the benchmarking data and FTEs used in the activities, extrapolation can be necessary for a small remainder of approximately 10–20%.

The main part of the as-is analysis is obviously the process discussion and documentation. It is useful to choose documentation tools that will be helpful. There is a range of tools to choose from, for instance:

- MS Office tools (PowerPoint, Excel, Word and so on).

- Process mapping tools, such as Visio, Optima, FlowCharter.

- Mapping and IT-integration tools, such as ARES, Accelerated SAP.

The decision must be based on the needs of the individual company. We find that in most cases Word or Excel are useful but insufficient alone. PowerPoint sometimes works, but in most cases is too simple for complex process-flow documentation. Visio and similar tools seem to work fine in most projects. Complex tools, such as ARES, that link with the ERP-system can be useful, if future documentation changes are anticipated to be very high. For small projects these tools are often too complex or require too many resources.

After choosing the tool set, the next problem is that:

- the required tools are possibly not available inside the company or there are not enough licences, or
- people participating in the project do not know the tools and need training on them.

The availability of the software should be included in the decision-making as a major criteria. It is better to take an existing tool that does the work, than discuss for months and procure a tool that does little more than the existing one but prolongs the project time-line and risks losing the momentum. Team up with IT to find a fast solution to installing the necessary tools on the project members' PCs.

Even if the tool selection and installation works fine (which hardly ever happens), the project members normally need training on using the tools. These trainings are elementary for success. The issues start with the fact that not everybody on the project has knowledge about process mapping, so the process-flow thinking itself is new. Training should include :

- process training on process flows in general;
- agreement and explanation of symbols to be used in process flow documentation;
- training on documentation structure (all different pieces of documentation and how they fit together);
- software functionalities (in the chosen tool);
- training on issues about working in a project (about communication necessity, keeping within time-lines, central documentation repository and so on).

All tools will produce process flows similar to that shown in Figure 41.

The set-up is always similar:

- There are so-called swim lanes per function or unit carrying out the activity (these can be horizontal or vertical, but are mostly horizontal).
- Symbols or shapes exhibit different meanings, such as activity, document, link.
- Individual boxes (activities) can be more sophisticated displaying IT system used as well as role behind activity.

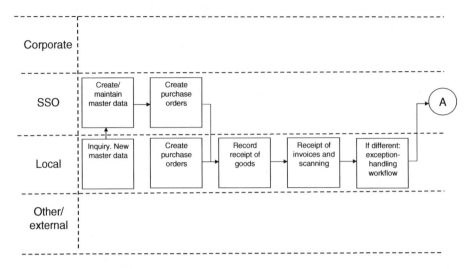

Figure 41   Flow chart example

The flow charts can look much more detailed and sophisticated. The basis for any process-flow documentation is an agreement on shapes and symbols to use. Figure 42 presents a complex example.

It is advisable to focus on as few shapes as possible, as the usage is otherwise too difficult for the newly trained project members.

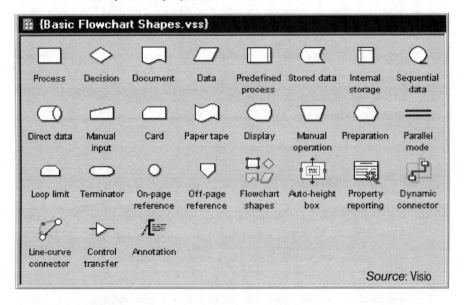

Figure 42   Example of shapes used: Visio

Documentation using process flows is not complete, however. It is necessary to have a repository for verbal explanations. This could be Word documents or a database, perhaps in Access, for example. The tool does not matter as long as it supports the documentation and does not become an end in itself. There might also be databases or lists for open issues, open 'to-do' reminders and so on. Complex projects will have several different documentation tools and a system and hierarchy behind them. The same system should be taken over later in the design phase.

To-be analysis

The to-be analysis is similar to the to-be design, which will be carried out in the design phase. However, in the feasibility study there is no need to design the future processes in too much detail yet, as there is no decision as regards carrying on with the SSO idea until the end of the feasibility phase. Hence, the to-be analysis is a similar thinking and drafting exercise, where the future processes are thought about, but on a higher level.

During the to-be analysis, it is possible to use process flows; but we recommend doing this only if the IT landscape is homogeneous and the process flows can be easily changed and transported to the future organization design. In most cases, though, IT is very diverse and detailed to-be design is not useful in this phase. Therefore, a list of best practices might be more useful to get an idea about improvement areas. It is important to remember that the to-be analysis has the purpose of understanding the as-is processes and the benchmarking figures in terms of potential improvement areas: the purpose is not yet the redesign.

A best-practice overview could look similar to the excerpt from a US chemical company's European operations shown in Table 46. The main point of the to-be analysis is to bring together the as-is process knowledge and the benchmarking knowledge and think about the improvement potentials and whether numeric results from benchmarking, for instance 50% savings potential, can really be done and what the changes would have to be to get there. This activity is a type of commonsense validation of the underlying data. It also saves project members from embarrassments that are possible if calculations are not really understood and then presented.

Definition of process split (central–local)

A very concrete result necessary for the business-case calculation is the estimate about the percentage of FTEs that can be transferred from local sites to the SSO, wherever that might be. To come up with this figure, it is necessary to track the individual activities and the respective FTEs connected to them and decide, activity by activity, whether each can be moved to a central location or not. The site visits with local finance people will be a good source of information regarding reasons why the process

Table 46   Best-practices usage overview – example

Best practices	France	Italy	Germany	UK	First quartile
Credit					
• Online view of consolidated customer sales, payment history and ageing across all business units	None	None	None	None	High
• Credit updates from third-party credit bureaux received electronically	None	None	None	None	65%
• Extent that credit-approval notification is sent back to customers via an Internet or intranet application	None	None	None	None	High
• Expediency in completing new credit reviews	Not avail.	Not avail.	Not avail.	Not avail.	High
Collection					
• Low percentage of aged invoices that are the result of internal errors made during the selling process	Not avail.	1%	Not avail.	18.5%	1%
• Extent finance has a formal performance management process to track, target and resolve root causes which delay payments	Not exist.	Not exist.	Not exist.	Not exist.	Not exist.
• Extent that the Internet or an intranet is utilized to automatically communicate with customers regarding past due accounts	N/a	N/a	N/a	N/a	Medium
• Optimized average monthly days sales outstanding (DSO)	90 days	153 days	36 days	77 days	41 days

cannot be moved. The result of this exercise will be that the 80–20 rule holds true. At least on average, 80% of the activities can be performed centrally, 20% need to remain local. The percentages for this 'central–local split' vary by process and by company. In some companies general ledger can be more difficult to move to an SSO. At the end the percentage in GL often is only 40–60%. In AP and AR the percentage can be 90% or more, although some companies come to the conclusion that they do not want to move AR at all. This depends a lot on the individual company. AP can be transferred almost always and mostly has a central–local–split with the central piece reaching 90% or more. An example from a life science company is shown in Table 47.

Table 47   Central–local split – example

	SSO (%)	Local (%)
Accounts payable	93	7
T&E accounting	81	19
Fixed assets	78	22
General accounting	80	20
Sales administration	89	11
Accounts receivable	92	8
Total	*82*	*18*

Another example from a retail company is shown in Table 48. The process areas in scope are somewhat different from the above example due to the specific industry. Also, the central–local split can be reviewed separately for the whole process scope and for the part of the process that runs through the finance function (see Table 49). This will exhibit some of the differences.

Table 48   Proposed total process split – example

Processes	SSO (%)	Local (%)
Fixed assets	100	0
General ledger	52	48
Accounts payable	87	13
Accounts receivable	36	64
Materials management	18	82
Outlet accounting	71	29
Total	*59*	*41*

Overall, the central–local split is approximately 60–40 but inside the finance function the respective split is nearly 90–10. Results such as these often have some political effects built into them, especially regarding the process parts outside of finance. Without politics, those percentages could have been higher but not as high as inside finance. These percentages are based on a detailed list of activities to be performed locally and centrally and link to the process flows.

Table 49   Proposed process split inside finance – example

Processes	SSO (%)	Local (%)
Fixed assets	100	0
General ledger	52	48
Accounts payable	87	13
Accounts receivable	100	0
Materials management	100	0
Outlet accounting	100	0
Total	*89*	*11*

Effects on people

A shared service project is mainly a change management issue, even though most companies concentrate on the IT and process issues. The SSO will have people in it who need to perform activities at specified performance levels so the success of the project depends on people. Since the effects on some people are negative, it is useful to spend some time in the feasibility study thinking about the effects on people and how to manage them. An industrial manufacturing company defined the CSFs of the SSO project to be 40% dependent on the change management work, 30% on board commitment and the last 30% only on process and IT design and implementation.

The initial effects on people are their fears about the project itself. That must be handled by a well-managed communication strategy. The other people issue is the question that everyone has in terms of 'what does that mean for me?'. It must be addressed and answered. Also, the project results in terms of FTE movements have to be translated into real person effects. The result of the feasibility will in most cases be that:

- some people remain locally at their jobs but may change roles;
- some people could move to the centre;
- some people are not needed in the future, but some of them might be needed during the project.

It is useful to not discuss any assumptions until the business case has been accepted. After that, the employees should get the true story. At the end, all people will have to be categorized into three categories:

- those needed in the future
- those needed for project duration but not after that
- those not needed in the future.

The first two groups must be actively secured as employees, as these are normally those people who would find other jobs too. To secure the second group's participation, incentives might be necessary. It is not uncommon to pay significant bonuses for those who stay for one to two years to support the transfer and then provide support in outplacement. If sold in the right way, most will accept such a solution.

Change management and communication

What is CHANGE MANAGEMENT?

Change management is the proactive planning and execution of specific activities to ensure participation and buy-in, reduce resistance, and increase the speed of acceptance. Such planning is essential when an organization makes changes to work processes or introduces new technology because the only way re-engineered processes, new technology, or any other change gets implemented is through people.

Experience and research have shown that many change efforts fail, are partially implemented or do not produce the cost savings or productivity increases anticipated. Beautifully designed processes go unused, and expensive information technology sits idle. People continue to use old processes and systems, and leaders move on to the next initiative or programme because the organization and people systems have not been designed to support and prepare employees and managers to function successfully in the end-state work environment.

Research and experience show that best-practice organizations realize this and utilize communication, teamwork, employee participation and training and development processes as a way to successfully transition the organization to the desired end state. By proactively analysing and managing the people and organizational factors, you increase your chances for success.

Based on this knowledge, the best advice is that change management be treated as a formal work thread integrated with the overall project plan and positioned within the project management office. Some key components of the general change management methodology include:

- change readiness assessment

- stakeholder analysis

- detailed planning (includes communication and training)

- change champion programme.

This methodology must be linked with the SSO project plan and used as necessary and applicable. Change management activities inside the SSO project in one practical example included the following range of topics:

- change management planning
- change enabling
- organizational change
- communication, motivation and mind-set
- skill analysis
- training and career development.

These topics will be relevant both in the feasibility phase as well as later phases. All topics could be discussed in length, but out of these topics communication in particular is essential in the feasibility phase. It is useful to explain that a feasibility really *is* a feasibility and people should participate and share all their worries so that the decisions can be based on more transparent data and information. Inside the change activities the main issue is that the project team and the management have just one chance to communicate well. If you miss that one chance, it will be difficult to correct later.

One should also consider that more people are interested in the project than just the project members; for example, if one employee participates in the project another employee must take over that person's job. Hence the person taking over is interested in why he or she must take over the colleague's job. Usually the communication is not prepared very well and regarded as not critical, even irrelevant. Hence the request from us to take it seriously. As an example of a detailed task list, a communication plan should be set up including something like this:

- Review existing information on change and communication.
- Set up communication strategy which is linked to relevant projects.
- Define communication vehicles for sending messages to and receiving feedback from stakeholders (central point-of-contact for query handling, FAQ documents, e-mail, hotline, newsletter, and so on).
- Develop communication plan linked to project phases (for example an event, stakeholder, communication owner, vehicle, frequency, location, message/purpose).
- Execute communication plan (project flyer, newsletter, hotlines, workshops).

- Provide means for employee feedback (raising issues, asking questions) and response, and address effectively and improve communication for further phases if necessary.

- Perform communication survey at end of each project phase (to determine whether or not communication has been effective).

- Identify motivation needs.

- Assess mind-set trainings (such as icebreakers, events).

Guiding principles in setting up communications are worth discussing in any project. An example from a US hospitality company looks like this:

- Communicate through people who are engaged in the project and who are able to demonstrate commitment to its vision.

- Provide effective two-way communication channels to ensure that the 'voice of the stakeholders' is heard and effectively addressed.

- Tailor the use of communication channels and vehicles to the needs and issues of specific stakeholders.

- Involve senior executive management in the communication process to foster credibility and associate trust in the change process.

- Leverage existing communication channels which are supplemented by additional channels as needed to achieve the project's goals.

- Create a 'marketing campaign' atmosphere over the life of the project designed to promote dialogue around the change with an ultimate goal of successful implementation and achievement of benefits.

- Align communications to project milestones in order to provide relevant information to stakeholders as the project progresses.

- Deliver messages using multiple channels and repeat messages to ensure that information is received and understood.

- Monitor feedback constantly and adjust communication accordingly in response.

The main task of the communication is to change people's thinking. In the change management cycle, thinking is the basis for feelings, behaviours and results. As we target specific results, the main goal is to identify change leaders and influence the thinking in the company in order to get the targeted results: support for the SSO and the successful implementation of the SSO. In terms of using any change management methodology we advise that the following summary on practical experiences is considered.

Change management is often defined as all change-related work including change leadership. It incorporates a wide range of views and activities. It is important to select the activities that are most promising in arriving at the set goals. It is also important to keep in mind some basic rules in performing change management:

- Methodology is a guide, not the answer:
  - focus on results and use methodology to guide you there
  - there are paths of least resistance – finding them is key
  - customize methodologies to your needs.

- There is an 80–20 rule with any project management:
  - define what is 'enough' – not what is 'more'
  - get out of the 'hope' and 'when' business.

- Intuition plays as strong a role as project management and methodology:
  - change requires relying on intuition when faced with the unknown
  - micro-management, sticking to methodology and endless analysis are cover-ups for fear of change.

IT ANALYSIS

The feasibility study always includes an IT analysis of some kind. These analyses can vary significantly in detail, but the minimum necessary is an overview on the IT landscape which could be just a list of sites and the IT systems used at those sites, perhaps for accounting and for other functions. A more substantiated analysis will include all relevant IT issues, as in the example shown in Figure 43.

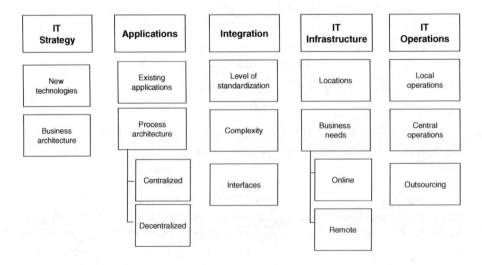

Figure 43   Aspects of IT analysis

The result of the IT analysis is, at least:

- understanding of current state in general, for example, how integrated is the IT platform?

- what potentials exist for IT standardization that support process optimization?

- what show stoppers exist on the IT side?

Hackett research has shown that integration and standardization are key in the IT environment of shared services:

- One hundred per cent of companies that are first quartile in benchmarking have one ERP system; amongst average companies, 79% have one ERP system.

- The feeder ratio amongst first-quartile companies is 1.3 compared with 3.5 for average companies; in other words, there are also less additional systems per primary application in a first-quartile company than in an average company.

The goal therefore must be to standardize the IT platform to be able to give best-practice support to the finance function and enable the finance function to move to first quartile themselves.

IT cooperation in the project

Finance people often have the view that the SSO project will be run by finance people and will produce some results that then must be implemented by IT people. This is only partly true. SSO is a project that should be run under the leadership of finance but must be a cooperative effort of both finance and IT people. Project management tends to try to split activities to reduce complexity of a big project. This is understandable but the problem is the 'putting together the puzzle' at the end. We strongly advise not splitting the teams into finance design teams and IT implementation teams but to combine finance and IT people in process teams and have them work together from feasibility to implementation.

Inside the teams there will always be a gap in knowledge, terminology and so on that must be bridged by someone. Practically this has to be done by finance: the finance people in the project must explain what they want using IT terminology. Hence, the process analysis has to include information about IT functionalities, ERP modules used, workflow tools, databases used and so on, so that the linkage with the results of the IT analysis is possible. In terms of the project organization, the process teams could be run like a tandem bicycle with a finance person in charge and an IT person as 'deputy'. IT personnel should be actively participating within the teams in any case.

IT effects on the finance SSO business case

SSO business cases are often built up based on a strict separation from IT and based on a range of assumptions about the IT effects on the IT landscape. Naturally, the current IT platform is known to the project members but in diversified IT environments some assumptions about future IT projects and the anticipated timing of the availability of a standardized platform might be necessary. The assumptions as such are not that problematic. The difficulty is often in the scoping. The IT projects are calculated based on their own business cases. The finance SSO again is a business case of its own. Both business cases assume effects from the other project. The first check is about whether these assumptions match and whether benefits and costs in both business cases have been included and included only and exactly once.

The next issue is one based on commonsense. As an example look at the IT cost budget and its development over time in Figure 44.

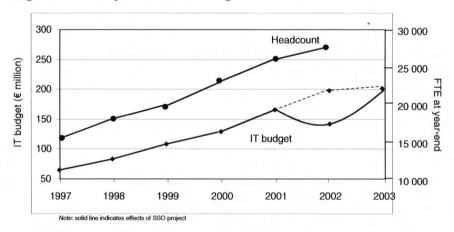

Figure 44   SSO benefit in avoiding additional IT cost

The IT budget in this example has been increasing by €20–30 million per year. The explanation of the IT budget growing relative to the number of employees does not have a logical base to it. There should not be a relation like this, but that is not the main issue. The main issue is that, in this example, the effects of the SSO project on the IT maintenance and operations cost would have been the ones exhibited by the solid line; in other words, IT costs would have been reduced significantly if there were only one platform instead of many. The dotted line exhibits the expected development without one single platform. Now, these savings were not included in the benefits of the finance SSO business case as they appear in IT, but they are only possible based on the collaboration of both functions. Also, the finance SSO business case must be considered bearing in mind that such benefits in other areas that might not appear in the business case but will appear as benefits for the company as a whole; in other words, there needs to be a kind of total company business-case view on all the individual business cases. Otherwise the scoping of the individual business cases can influence their results and lead to misinterpretation and wrong decisions.

An effect often misinterpreted in business cases is the effect of IT on future finance cost. All business cases are built on cost savings: actual reductions of running annual costs. However, in many cases, as explained above, there are well-founded expectations that costs will rise in the future and certain activities – the set-up of an SSO – can reduce the growth of costs. Finance costs could be assumed to grow relative to the company's revenues. If an SSO is built, the costs would actually decrease. The benefit from this should be calculated as two components:

- actual savings (future cost minus current actual cost)

- avoided costs (those costs that would have occurred without the measures taken).

The sum of these two are the total financial benefits. Let us take the example of a telecommunications company. Working in dollars, the run rate savings would have been $9 million ($26 million existing cost minus $17 million existing future costs). The actual benefit though is $54 million, based on the assumed cost increase in the old environment, because costs would have increased to $71 million if they were assumed to grow relative to company revenue.

The inclusion of avoided costs into business cases is something that the company's top management must allow and do based on commonsense and possibly in deviation from investment calculation formats. External consultants, project members or the finance function will not promise these 'savings' as they cannot 'deliver' them inside their responsibility area and IT will not 'take over' responsibility for savings calculated based on an 'outside' business case.

LOCATION ANALYSIS

This is the one topic that 'makes the masses move'. Everybody is interested in the location selection and has a huge list of opinions and arguments. This is the one topic where mobilizing participation will not be necessary. It is necessary to understand the following base terminology: the feasibility phase includes the work package 'location analysis', which actually includes four activity parts, all of which are normally performed within the feasibility study in this order:

- location analysis
- location selection
- site analysis
- site selection.

The location analysis would always start by looking at continents and countries and then narrow down the view angle; but, in general, when referring to a location, we mean something smaller than a country, normally a city, possibly an area (for example, Bay Area, Greater London) or region (for example, Midlands). A site is normally defined more closely as being the actual property or even building chosen. Naturally there is always an analysis and then a decision, a selection made. The location analysis and selection is by far the more exciting piece of work and also the one requiring significant resources, just because of the lengthy political discussions often necessary.

Whatever the geographical scope of the location analysis is, the methodology is always similar:

1. *Overall assessment:* evaluation of market data, best practices and so on.

2. *Longlist:* there will be a list of 10–15 locations that make sense.

3. *Shortlist:* the actual assessment with more detailed criteria to reduce the longlist to between two and five remaining candidates.

4. *Location selection:* choose one from the shortlist.

5. *Site analysis and selection:* look for suitable property and building in the city of choice.

After that, operational location build-up will take place (in design and implementation phases), if the feasibility study is successful and the SSO is built. In some cases, only the location selection is made during the feasibility study and the site analysis and selection are performed during design. Key selection criteria in the location analysis include:

- total cost of ownership
- risk mitigation
- business supportability
- speed to implementation
- intangibles.

Let's further understand the importance of each of these key selection criteria and some of the details which comprise them.

Total cost of ownership

The ability to achieve substantial cost savings continues to be the single most important reason behind the move to shared services. Therefore, a solid business case is crucial to the overall success of the shared services and the location decision. Past efforts to value the move to shared services have focused on the cost of implementation and the required payback period. In our client work, we have found that the total cost of ownership (TCO) approach, coupled with a shareholder value analysis (such as EVA), allows for the true impact of shared services decisions to be on the corporation. Key components of the shared services location decision business-case analysis include:

- Implementation and one-time costs:
  - hardware/software
  - telecommunications
  - relocation and separation expenses
  - recruiting and training fees
  - facility build-out cost
  - current lease termination cost
  - moving expenses.

- Ongoing operating costs:
  - labour and fringe (managers, professionals, clerical) – probably the single most important aspect of the site-selection decision
  - facilities (lease or allocated cost) – will vary substantially from location to location
  - services (power, telecommunications and so on)
  - IT infrastructure support.

- Additional savings/incentives:
  - industrial development incentives
  - tax incentives, local, state, provincial, and so on.

This list will vary from company to company and the criteria need to be weighted to reflect the individual targets and the chosen approach.

Many local governments are eager to attract new business to their areas and often reward decisions to locate in their cities in the form of business – and property – tax concessions. Additionally, these local governments can offer subsidies for training, construction and set-up costs. These subsidies often come in the form of further tax concessions and grants. These savings can be substantial and should be a key component of the business case. However, since many of these tax incentives can be discussed, it is also important to compare locations first based on other criteria and then add the tax incentives at the end for those locations selected based on the remaining criteria. Our experience is that maybe one third of the companies we worked with in connection with an SSO viewed taxes and local government incentives as key drivers of their location decision.

Many cities, states and countries are eager to have new businesses in their locations and are willing to negotiate significant reductions in business and property taxes, which can add up to millions of dollars in savings. In Europe, as an example, certain countries (including Belgium, Ireland, the Czech Republic, Netherlands, the UK, Wales and Denmark) have special SSO incentive programmes. But even those that don't have special programmes will be willing to hold discussions when confronted with the location selection criteria and options. Examples of tax benefits in Europe are:

- Tax holidays: 10% ten-year corporate-tax rate in Ireland for new investments, or Swiss cities and cantons offering even lower rates.

- The Mezzo-Giorno in Italy offers lower social-security taxes, as do certain Spanish regions.

- Belgium offers attractive expatriate packages with reduced income taxation, for example for those relocating to Belgium as SSC management.

- East European countries have appealing general income-tax rates, such as Slovakia at 19%.

The business-case analysis framework should also include key valuation criteria such as:

- savings

- one-time implementation costs

- incremental cashflow improvements of each location

- NPV of incremental cashflows of each location

- shareholder value metric (for example EVA).

Risk mitigation

While locating the new shared services organization in a greenfield location allows for a unique/success-oriented organizational culture to be created, it does present risk. Some of these risks include:

- Support availability:
  - HR support capabilities

  - existing IT support capabilities
  - telecom 'last mile' reliability and coverage
  - cost of redundancy (severance cost).

- Ability to leverage staff and facilities:
  - availability of in-scope staff to relocate, if necessary, to the new location
  - existing knowledge of legacy technology and processes
  - existing knowledge of regulatory requirements (GAAP, IFRS, and so on).

- Shared services organization design:
  - ability to accept the new SSO design and to subsequently establish it.

A detailed risk-mitigation plan is important. This plan should quantify each risk (for example, as a percentage reduction in savings and/or percentage increase in cost) as part of the overall business case in order that the best overall decision is facilitated.

Business supportability

Next to cost, the quality and skill of the local workforce is one of the most critical location decision factors to be made. Greenfield locations often reflect a cost advantage over locations near existing facilities (brownfield locations) but typically carry a higher risk. Simply consolidating general and administrative (G&A) personnel to save money is nothing more than centralization. Therefore, the two drivers (cost savings and quality/skill of the staff) is crucial to building a customer-centric shared services organization.

Additionally, it is important to look at other aspects of the new location such as the saturation of the local labour market, labour costs in existing industries, the employment rate and workforce turnover. These indicators can provide helpful insight into the further benefits (or negative impacts) of each location under consideration. Further analysis criteria include:

- Workforce factors:
  - regional wage structure(s) – managers, professionals, clerical
  - skilled workforce availability, demographics, skill set
  - competition for workforce
  - education of available workforce
  - workforce turnover statistics
  - workforce performance data
  - presence of other companies (Fortune 500, Global Titans and so on)
  - universities
  - work ethic/productivity
  - population/projected employment market
  - unemployment rate.

- Geographic factors:
  - proximity to company headquarters and other locations
  - location accessibility (via aeroplanes, trains, and so on).

- Culture and language factors:
  - language availability
  - ease in adapting to different cultures.

English is the predominant language; however, other languages might be as or more important depending on the service scope of the individual SSC. For the Americas, Spanish is often important when the SSC will serve customers, vendors and/or employees in markets where the Spanish language is required and/or seen as a market advantage. North American locations with low labour costs and an abundance of multilingual employees often serve Central and South American locations where local business operations in that country would accommodate consolidated sourcing of services. In Europe, German, English, French, Russian or Italian might be the key language for a regional SSC. In many cases English will not be sufficient. In Asia, different types of Chinese might be critical but if the scope is more Pacific than Asian, English might do.

In Europe different countries have different cultures resulting in different working cultures. The work–life balance can vary significantly, in terms of expectations about what that should look like. As a result, working-time issues have to be balanced against time-zone issues that can come up depending on the scope of the SSC. Europe has at least three time zones to cover, the US has five and an Asian centre would possibly need to cover even more time zones, depending on the scope.

Speed to implementation

Once management has made the decision to move to a shared services model, the need to move quickly is important. Therefore, the ability for the new shared services organization to 'get up to speed' and begin realizing the benefits outlined in the business case is critical and should be one of the prime decision criteria. Greenfield locations frequently present substantial lease/rent as well as facility cost savings. While these factors should be seriously considered when making the location decision, availability at the time required can often present a challenge. Locating near existing company operations (brownfield site) has the advantage of access to an existing skilled labour pool, which will be fully up to speed with company procedures and culture. As a result, training and associated costs are less than at a greenfield site. The demands on the change management aspect of the project will also be reduced, with the amount of upheaval being minimized by the use of existing facilities. The following 'people and facility factors' should be considered when making the location decision:

- People factors:
  - availability of skilled resources (labour and fringe costs)
  - knowledge of processes in scope to shared services
  - time required to transition to shared services
  - perception, by the business units, about workforce skill/quality.

- Facility factors:
  - office-space quality, availability and rates
  - telecommunications quality and availability
  - time to acquire and prepare facility.

Intangibles

The local business infrastructure is typically not a concern within Western countries such as Western Europe, the US, Canada, Japan, Hong Kong or Australia, but can be a concern if one of the shared service sites under consideration is located in Central or South America, Eastern Europe, parts of Asia or Africa. However, there are several criteria that should be factored into the decision such as public transportation, cost of housing (if relocation is a key element), local or municipal government incentives and/or tax concessions, available grants as well as quality-of-life considerations. The following represent some of the criteria that should be considered:

- Overall business environment (pro-business, family-owned, philanthropic, community perception, and so on):
  - local infrastructure
  - power availability and reliability
  - availability of water, gas and other utilities
  - public and private transportation
  - home affordability
  - state income tax
  - political and economic stability of area
  - incentives and subsidies
  - grants from government
  - tax concessions
  - receptiveness of state and local governments.

- Quality of life:
  - cost of living/climate/crime rate
  - primary and secondary education quality
  - recreational and social environment
  - transportation and traffic trends.

The impact of these intangibles can often be critical 'knock-out' criteria to the location decision.

In summary, developing a comprehensive and unbiased business case is of utmost importance to the acceptance of the shared service organization within the company. The location decision can serve as a positive 'kick-start' to the new organization. A thorough analysis of the costs and benefits of each location is important to the decision process as any business-case scenario will always be location-dependent: in other words, the same scenario will have different results when based on location data for different cities.

In terms of advice and best practices, there are many things to consider and every location analysis is different. A summary of some of the location wisdom, beneficial behaviours, criteria to consider include:

- Many companies have a global SSO but no organization has established a truly global SSC. It is probably possible, but barriers so far have included:
  - language
  - regulatory environment
  - culture.

- Currently, common practice is to establish regional centres in North America; Latin America (often colocated with the North American SSC); Europe, the Middle East and Africa (EMEA); the Pacific Rim/Asia.

- Brownfield – reduced risk but sub-optimized financial benefits.

- Greenfield – lower cost, addresses opportunity to create unique culture, maximize financial benefits.

- Quality-of-life issues are growing in importance – the ability to attract employees and retain them in an ever-increasing competitive global environment increases in importance and is a basic requirement for sustainable solution.

- A location is optimal for a fixed period of time, say three to five years. After that relocation might be necessary. Hence planning and payback should not be longer.

- Consider at least one 'wild card' greenfield location as a 'hidden gem'.

- Emphasis in the future will be on skills of people resulting in the necessity to balance quality against costs.

- Location complexity will increase.

- Location needs to serve as a platform for future growth.

- Focus on education systems and customer-service attitudes.

- Ultimately, people will make the difference.

- Choices – establish a new culture or change the old one.

- It is difficult to establish customer-service attitude with people who came from a centralized staff group.

- Always finish the location selection process with one chosen location and one back-up location. Possibly short-term issues (such as the co-location of other large SSCs in the same city at the same time producing a labour shortage) will require fast rethinking.

Location analysis results

The summary results of the location analysis work can be displayed in very different forms. One possibility is exhibiting quantitative and qualitative benefits and costs in a so-called cost-quality matrix or trade-off matrix, as in Figure 45. Figure 45 shows how much certain cities deviate from a theoretical average line (left top to right bottom) and thereby how much better (above) or worse they are. In this case cities 3, 4 and 5 would have the best chances.

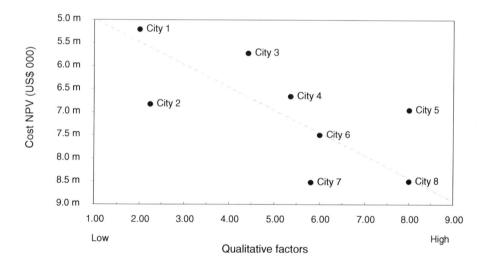

Figure 45   Example of 'trade-off matrix'

A cost analysis can be broken into cost components and compared for one scenario with different location alternatives. Table 50 presents a US example.

The summary results regarding the location would be some kind of two-dimensional comparisons with actual figures for cost and savings, possibly also IIR and NPV. The format could be as shown in Figure 46. These comparisons are naturally dependent on the company-specific criteria weighting and the time of calculation.

Table 50   Example – total location cost analysis

	One-time implementation cost in US$million	Salary and benefits in US$million	Facilities' lease in US$million	Total operating cost (five-year horizon) in US$ million
White plains	3.1	17.7	0.1	20.9
Location B	3.8	20.1	1.1	25.0
Location C	4.1	18.3	1.1	23.5
Madison	4.0	16.0	0	20.0
Norfolk	4.1	15.9	1.5	21.5
Phoenix	4.1	16.1	1.1	21.3
Fargo	3.9	12.9	1.0	17.8

The attractiveness of certain cities does change over time, so analyses done some years ago are, for most locations, no longer valid and need to be recalculated.

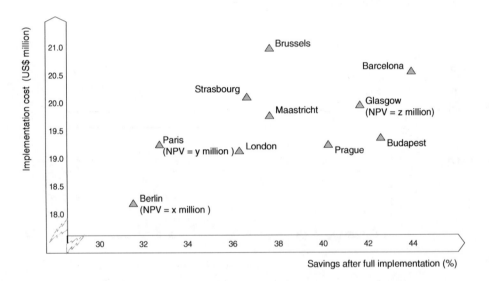

Figure 46   Financial location analysis (including summary of costs, savings and NPV per location

LEGAL AND REGULATORY ISSUES

Several companies spend a lot of effort on the analyses of legal and regulatory issues. This block, sometimes referred to as issues of government, comprises all issues around:

- a legal framework
- a regulatory framework
- tax legislation.

The assessment itself is normally carried out in two steps:

- Connected with location analysis work, longlist locations will be assessed by high-level review in terms of show stoppers: reasons strictly prohibiting the company from choosing that location.

- Shortlisted or chosen locations will be assessed in more detail, say in terms of the legal environment for setting up a legal entity in that country.

In some of the more 'aggressive' approaches, the SSO solution is built around the general rule that:

- everything useful and beneficial will be done, everything will be standardized, there is always one system and one way to do things at best-practice level;

- the only allowed exception is the legal necessity to do something different.

If one takes such a view, it is very important to separate business and culture issues from those issues that have actual legal background. In many companies people will tell you hundreds of reasons why an SSO cannot work. In the site visits you can collect a list of their fears. Most of them will be valid thoughts but also, in most cases, the issues are not legal but business or cultural. Nevertheless, there are enough legal issues, especially in Europe and Asia, to worry about. As an example, major categories of issues in Europe are:

- the local language/currency must be used in most countries
- the local GAAP must be respected
- quick accessibility to books and documents must be possible in case of tax audits
- an active terminal to have access to a computerized system is required in most countries.

Some countries are 'more difficult' than others, but issues are often very diverse, so a general 'black list' will not be very helpful, as the biggest regulatory issues a specific country has might not be of relevance to a specific company. Some examples of regulatory issues are:

- In certain countries, such as Germany, the commercial law provides no issues against SSO but the German Tax Act disallows transfer of 'booking decisions' to a location outside Germany; however, exceptions are possible. Poland has similar restrictions.

- Some national regulations require local hardware, an example being Sweden, where since 2000 hardware used for booking must be located in Sweden. Exemptions are possible especially for foreign-owned companies.

- Some countries demand a legally binding chart of accounts: in Greece the ledgers, the booking sequence, the numbering and the account descriptions are mandated.

- These may be process-specific restrictions, such as:
  - local approval of T&E required
  - cash movements restricted or complicated, as in Italy
  - certain professional fees in France require income tax to be withheld and paid by the party buying the service
  - self-billing is illegal in certain countries (despite EU regulations).

- Other continents than Europe have regulatory issues too. In the US there are 50 different state sales taxes running between approximately 0–10% and changing over time.

There are issues which are results of regulatory issues such as in Greece, where certain IT platforms are not supported by the vendor (for example SAP R/3 4.6b vs. 4.6c for Greece). These could be also categorized as legal issues.

There are hundreds, maybe thousands of legal issues. The main point, though, is that:

- there are very few show stoppers or reasons not to go on with the SSO project;

- there is a list of issues that need to be solved and can be solved in parallel to the remaining project moving on;

- if there are too many issues in one country, it can be useful to reduce the scope (taking that country out of scope) because the benefits might not pay for all the issue-resolution work (the 'workarounds' possible).

A consumer-goods company eliminated Greece from its European SSO scope because of legal issues. This company was able to include Poland, France, Italy and Russia, though. A water purification company was able to include all of Europe as well as Middle Eastern countries (Saudi Arabia and Kuwait) and Caucasian countries

(Azerbaijan). Two years later the SSO collapsed because benefits did not materialize. Several companies have moved countries such as Italy, France, Poland, Russia, Greece and Turkey to the end of the implementation timetable. Legal advisors often state Greece and Poland to be impossible to include.

In Australasia and Asia, the listing will be of similar importance and structure as in Europe. Certain countries – Australia, New Zealand, Singapore and India – are not big issues. Others – Japan, Thailand and China – can be tricky. Issues in the legal area will change even faster than in Europe: in China regulation changes extremely fast, especially after the country joined the WTO in 2003.

The legal and regulatory environment must also be seen from a stability and security point of view. Some 60% of worldwide tax literature is in German. This is a clear indication of over-regulation. On the other hand, there has been clarity and stability in the structures, whether deemed good or bad.

Political stability, assessed under location analysis, can also have an influence on legal and regulatory frameworks. Whereas legal systems in Peru and Colombia have become unattractive compared to their standing some 20–30 years ago, the opposite is the case for Russia, China and many Arab countries.

Companies operating globally know that the international exposure creates a legal minefield. The best advice is to get transparency on the legal issues. Often it is possible to discuss solutions with local authorities. It is not acceptable to block the SSO project because of legal issues as there is enough proof of solutions. With Sarbanes-Oxley Act and similar legislation in place or to come into force in other countries, legal issues are increased in importance again and will require more time and resource effort to deal with.

SCENARIO DEVELOPMENT AND ASSESSMENT

The scenario development and assessment builds on the scenario work done in Phase Zero (high-level scenario development) and on all the previous work steps in Phase One. The scenario discussion is in a way a summary of the work results and the structuring of results. The main focus is on developing scenarios. These are necessary, because the amount of theoretically possible alternatives and combinations of criteria are endless. Every company needs to agree a list of scenarios that are then evaluated.

The approach is in some ways similar to the location assessment. There can be a first longlist of a large number of scenarios, more or less all the possible solutions. This list would be reduced immediately by:

- scenarios outside the scope;

- scenarios regarded undesirable or useless (only those where it is sure they will not be interesting to anybody);

- scenarios regarded politically unstable (should be used carefully, as some comparisons might be helpful for transparency reasons).

The list will still be long – maybe hundreds of scenarios. They are only described in terms of 'SSO for transactional finance only, Western Europe, one SSC, old systems' or similar. The next step is to reduce them to a workable number, normally five to ten scenarios. The options map, explained in Phase Zero, could be used again. An important input is the assumptions list, because it enables one to define scenarios with more detail. It is always possible to have loads of variations per scenario – they should be discussed but limited to a minimum for the actual assessment. The scenarios used must be described. Figure 47 is an example of a high-level description for a very small scope exercise.

There should generally be a more detailed description per scenario or it would be covered by detail in the assumptions list. A short list of scenarios then would be evaluated in terms of a list of defined criteria, such as that presented in Figure 48.

The shortlist evaluation can be done in several ways. A mathematical summary can also be given in terms of a total score. Some people like to be very analytic, some decide from gut instinct. Depending on the approach, the above content could be worked with in the opposite order too: there could be an assessment of a range of scenarios and then the chosen ones would be described in more detail. It is advisable to describe scenarios in as much detail as possible at the time of discussion so that those scenarios that are chosen also reflect the content people thought they were choosing.

The decision-making process on choosing scenarios can be very complicated. It is useful to engage as many stakeholders as possible in this part of the project. A scenario workshop including all project management members, the country CFOs and business-unit representatives plus IT and HR is a good starting team set-up to think about. In case of a pharmaceutical company, a scenario workshop with approximately 15 persons was carried out lasting two days. The discussion is difficult but it will deliver an agreement on the scenarios. The location issue, often discussed at the same workshop, will be even more exciting.

The scenario assessment will deliver evaluated scenarios and then link directly into the business-case calculation, as the business case really is nothing more than the sum of scenarios and their comparison. A single scenario could be displayed using the key metrics, like the example in Figure 49 from a US chemical company.

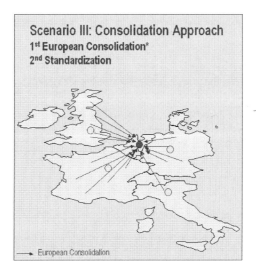

Figure 47   SSO business-case scenarios

Often scenarios can be agreed upon, but the locations may be fought about hard and the aggressiveness of the approach is difficult to agree upon. The CFO typically wants to move fast and get benefits even faster. Other project members and the local people opt for 'more evolutionary than revolutionary' approaches.

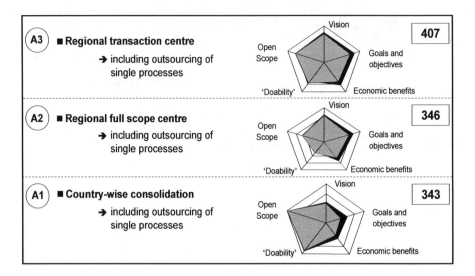

Figure 48   Example – short-list scenarios

Approach

The discussion about the approach is part of the scenario development and also a critical input for the business-case calculation. Depending on the chosen approach, results can vary significantly and even change around totally. There is a range of questions discussed in connection with the options map, but typically the approach discussion is only about a few decisions:

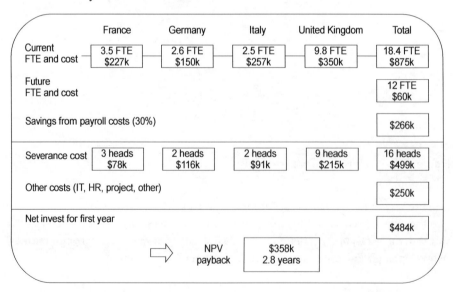

Figure 49   Scenario-analysis example: results from scenario 1 (best case)

- Standardize first or consolidate first?

- Move directly from one state to another (big bang) or take a phased approach?

The answers to these two questions will give you an approach.

In terms of the consolidation and standardization order question, it seems to be that some companies, such as GM, work well with the consolidation approach. The idea is to consolidate all resources to one SSC and then standardize in that one location. Clearly it is easier to standardize when all resources are in that location. In terms of implementation, this approach is always more of a big-bang approach. Other companies, such as Henkel, prefer the standardization approach, mainly because it allows them to go down the road of a phased approach, moving from several locations to possibly one SSC by moving in predefined steps over a longer time period. There is no right or wrong. There seems to be a link between the chosen solution and the company culture and current state. Companies that have good control over remote locations may try the phased approach. Companies that feel their locations are very independent and that standardization has little chance of succeeding try the consolidation approach more often. In some cases, political reasons make only one of the approaches possible.

The most important result to understand is that the phased approach will possibly be easier to follow with less pain attached to it, but naturally it will also deliver fewer benefits or at least take longer to deliver, hence almost always resulting in an NPV or whatever that is less attractive than in the consolidation approach. The reason is that in the phased approach, there is a significant amount of double-work. If the phased approach is chosen, it is important to choose exactly the 'highest possible hill to climb' (see Figure 50).

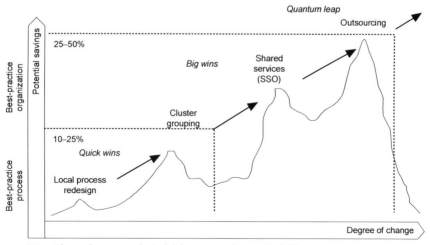

Figure 50   Phased approach: 'which mountain to climb?'

To change from a cluster to a global SSO is possible but requires significant rework that adds to the total workload. The additional work is the 'road down the hill and up again'.

An assessment of companies that have had an SSO for some time shows that those companies that went directly for outsourcing or a global SSO have had faster payback than companies that took the phased approach or that limited their scope, say to a national SSO (see Figure 51).

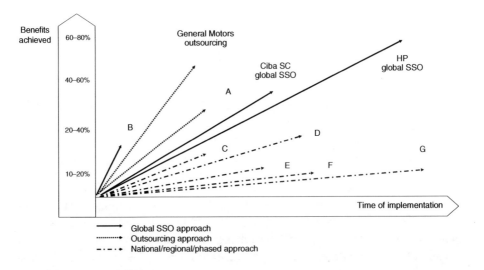

Figure 51   Benefits of different consolidation approaches

VERIFICATION OF OUTSOURCING OPTION AND OUTSOURCING VERSUS SSO

It is advisable to calculate one scenario for the outsourcing alternative, even if this is not wanted and maybe not even considered. The additional work is very limited when done in conjunction with the scenario assessment inside the feasibility study. The verification of the outsourcing option really only requires an additional scenario here, whereas later a separate assessment can be much more costly. Also, experience shows that at some point in time someone will ask why the outsourcing possibility was not looked at. It is useful then to have at least the comparable data available. The complete assessment of the outsourcing option will be more comprehensive: to validate the mathematical assessment you would actually need to discuss with some BPOs to get real-life offers. This would only be necessary though after a decision to consider outsourcing seriously.

We defined SSO as opposed to outsourcing at the beginning of this book. Of course we could do a comparison of them in terms of benefits too. In reality this is difficult, as the comparison must be based on individual companies. However, as a general guideline, here are some things to consider when evaluating internal SSOs against outsourcing:

- *Financials:* business case including investment and savings profile.

- *Quality:* expected quality gap (in BPO service) and necessity to maintain competencies.

- *Flexibility:* increase or decrease.

- *Best practices:* access to external know-how (best practice, benchmarking, market prices).

- *Organization and culture:* change readiness.

- *Process and IT platform:* cleaned-up and clearly defined.

- *Timing:* before or after completion of SSO.

Outsourcing has been around for some time and BPO should be considered an established and mature market. Every company has to decide if business risk and strategic importance of the content in scope are low – in that case the outsourcing will make sense (see Figure 52).

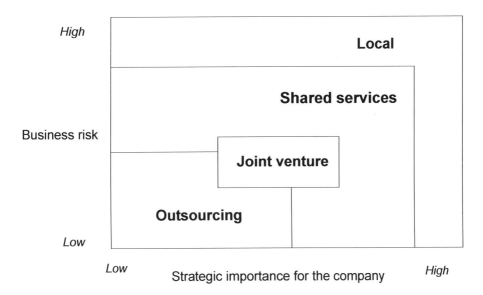

Figure 52   Internal shared services versus outsourcing

Even if individual companies decide against outsourcing, it is perceived as having a bright future. Annual growth numbers for the BPO business have been ranging between 15 and 50% in the past years. Strategically, this movement is just the prolongation of the core business thinking (see Figure 53).

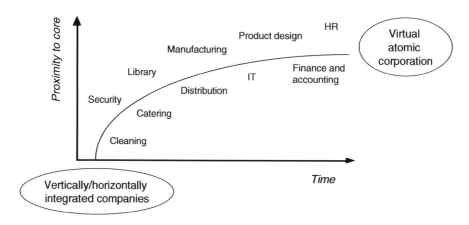

Figure 53   Outsourcing: the development

Most of us will still remember the fight about outsourcing catering or the car park. Today it is perceived as normal. As the topics in scope get closer to the core business the scoping and decision-making get more difficult but do not stop the trend. A representative from HP once summarized the perceived end of the road as: 'At the end there will be only two kinds of companies: those who outsource and those who are outsourcers.' If this holds true, the real question will be not whether to outsource but when to outsource.

This statement might be true, but for a certain scope. The discussion might be about what is the scope for which this statement holds true, say in terms of company size as in Figure 54.

It seems to be that outsourcing is well suited for both big and small organizations, but is not always easy to do for medium-sized businesses. Also, certain industries are better suited for it than others. Characteristics of applicable industries include:

- large cost base
- high growth
- high share of service processes
- high share of business-to-consumer processes.

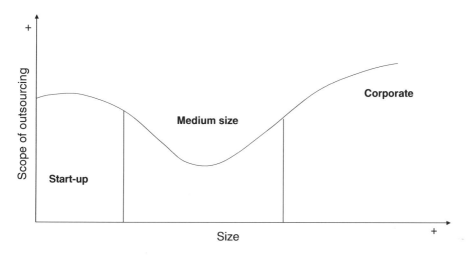

Figure 54   Outsourcing: relevant size of business

As a result, sectors such as hospitality, real estate and electronics are not that suited, while banking and insurance, car manufacturing and utilities are. Interestingly, the suitability is not always reflected in real-life results, because manufacturing and banking do use outsourcing heavily whereas utilities still lag behind. This is possibly a result of the former monopoly environment and will possibly change in the future.

Of course there are benefits and drawbacks that must be rated individually, but some general aspects include:

Potential drawbacks:

- less influence on 'internal processes'
- cultural change
- less influence on services provided
- less influence on employees
- danger/fear of loss of control and know-how
- quality of life
- cost.

Benefits:

- improved competitiveness
- increase of shareholder value
- access to and build-up of best practices
- flexibility
- focus on 'core' possibilities
- ability to plan and steer long-term cost
- 'guaranteed' re-engineering success.

It is not necessary to carry out the full assessment on outsourcing and the BPO market in the feasibility phase, but it is useful to have the necessary data available for comparisons, whether now or later. In the location analysis, the outsourcing scenario requires an additional assessment of the outsourcing capacity of the selected locations; in other words, are there free or potential BPO capacities available?

CONCEPTUAL SSO DESIGN

The detailed SSO design is not necessary in the feasibility phase – it will be done in Phase Two. Remember that we still do not have a positive decision in terms of continuing. It therefore does not make sense to go into too much detail in designing the SSO, yet.

The conceptual design of the SSO will develop in conjunction to the scenario discussion. Most answers will be given in the scenario development. For purposes of designing the structure, those results only need to be enhanced by some organizational thinking in terms of the future SSO and the SSC(s), such as in terms of staffing. It is helpful for the selling of the case to have actual names in the business case, even if it is just a best guess. It should demonstrate the availability of resources, the depth of thinking that went into the creation of the business case, and the key roles, for example the SSC director, should have been discussed with the candidates. This is also relevant for the business case, as an inability to select internal people will lead to more external cost for recruiting that must be built into the business case.

IMPLEMENTATION PLAN

One of the products of the feasibility study must be a plan about what to do. In this case it will be an implementation plan. For the purpose of selling the business case to colleagues and making a decision, the implementation plan only needs high-level content. If the business case is accepted, the selected scenario must be used for detailed planning. Naturally, the planning will be more precise for the design phase than for the phases thereafter. An example of a high-level planning for Phase Two looks like that shown in Figure 55.

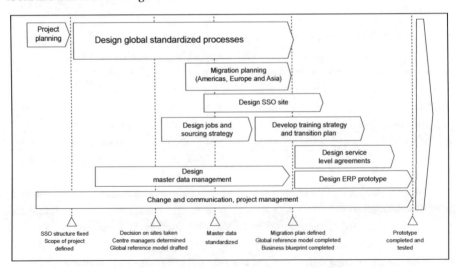

Figure 55   Outline project plan for Phase Two: design and construction

The implementation plan needs to consider the linkage with possible IT activities. If there is an IT migration plan, that will most certainly be a direct input to the implementation planning. Otherwise, possible future IT migrations also need to be considered, at least as options.

COST-BENEFIT ANALYSIS AND BUSINESS CASE

All results of the feasibility study culminate in the production of the business case, which really is the summary of all the components discussed and a quantitative summary and a recommendation or result. Normally the deliverable takes the form of a slide presentation. The scenario overview in the business case could look like the consumer-goods example shown in Table 51.

Table 51   Example – summary of business case results (list)

	NPV (US$mm)	Annual savings (US$mm)	Initial cost (US$mm)	Pay back (years)	Finance cost reduction (%)
Country consolidation	31.9	10.9	17	3	16.3
X related BUs	13.6	5.1	10.7	3	7.6
Regional transaction centre					
High-cost base	-0.3	10.1	33.8	6	15.2
Low-cost base	24.6	16.9	33.3	4	25.4
Regional full centre					
High-cost base – all BUs	-2	17.1	50.6	7	25.8
Low-cost base – all BUs	29.6	27.2	49.7	5	41.0
High-cost base	-5.4	11.8	36.3	7	17.7
Low-cost base	8.5	15.7	35.9	6	22.3
Regional full centre by BU	**9.2**	**14.8**	**47.2**	**5**	**22.3**

Note: Regional full-scope centre offers highest annual savings potential; however, at substantial cost and longer-term payback. Location is a key consideration. Country consolidations offer most attractive NPV with a three-year payback and create a basis for future regional consolidation. BU: business unit.

All numerical results can be displayed in graphical formats too. It is often useful to use both formats, as some people prefer reading numbers, some prefer pictures (see Figure 56).

The final recommendation can be just the selection of one scenario. It could also be that the recommended route is one using several scenarios and linking them in a

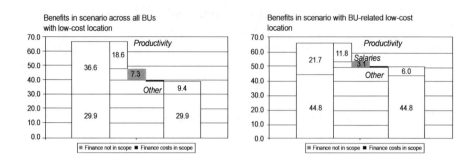

Figure 56   Example – summary business-case results (two scenarios)

phased approach; for instance, first a national SSO and then a regional SSO. In the example in Figure 57, the route could take one from scenario zero (S0) through scenario one to scenario five (S5). This route only incorporates process improvements and consolidation of selected companies into the SSC. After that a possible route of further opportunities could be national SSCs (O1) or one could go directly to regional SSCs (O2) that then lead to a global SSO (O3).

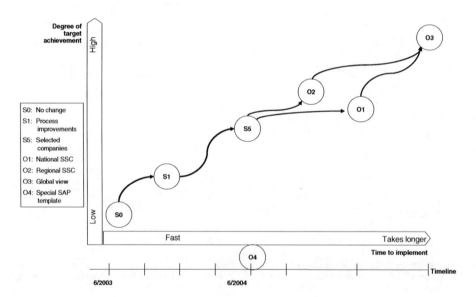

Figure 57   Phased implementation approach

CHAPTER 11

Design

RELEVANCE OF PHASE TWO IN RELATION TO CHOSEN APPROACH

If a company chooses to consolidate first and standardize thereafter, as was the case with GM, then the sequencing of the phases and the content will vary a little. Our phasing is based on the 'standard case'. In a strongly consolidation-driven approach, the activities inside Phases Two and Three will be mixed and carried out in the order best suited to the company. This will not change the fact that all content will be relevant as work packages, possibly with differing weighting though.

For some people it is not clear what the difference in content between these phases is. Some advisors seem also to mix them up or at least put everything in one basket. These were the high-level definitions to explain the differences in terms of goals and deliverables/results from one client example:

- Goal of feasibility study:
    - find out if centralized F&A organization makes sense for us in Europe
    - support the decision about future F&A organization in Europe
    - identify potentials for optimization in the processes.

- Goal of design and validation phase:
    - design the full set of best-practice processes for future F&A organization in Europe
    - validate these processes with the legal entities in Europe
    - create the baseline for the implementation to the future system architecture (blueprint).

- Results of feasibility study:
    - as-is analysis (selective)
    - benefit estimation for SSO
    - general to-be process ideas for major processes – KPI analysis, calculation of different scenarios, to-be process ideas
    - best practices as a list of different approaches
    - critical success factors.

- Results of design and validation phase:
    - detailed to-be design
    - validated standard processes for Europe with blueprint information (after validation)

> – design for best-practice processes – intelligent combination of all best practices into one process for Europe.

This is a company example so the respective bullets could look a bit different in another case, but the main line of thought should stay the same.

The big difference is that these activities take place *after the decision* to implement an SSO. Deciding to create an SSO is probably the easiest part of the build-up. Setting up a new organization is actually quite difficult and even though there is a decision to support the work, it is useful to try to stick to simple, lean, non-bureaucratic and value-adding principles.

DETAILED PROCESS DESIGN

The topic of detailed design is one which will be extremely important in real life, as the future SSO will work on the platform designed here. In terms of commenting, this is actually a phase which needs nothing else than resources and hard will to carry through the work. There are few tips in terms of reducing the work – the workload will have been determined by the work in the previous phases. The only thing left here is to 'just do it'.

The detailed design is based on the process design and documentation structure from Phase One. However, it needs to go into more detail. Here it is not sufficient to describe best-practice ideas: ERS, OCR, self-service, three-way matching and so forth. These ideas need to take up the form of detailed processes with an activity box for each activity and with clear links to the actually chosen IT platform in the form of naming the functionality of that ERP module or the IT tool used. The design will be more detailed than the one exhibited in Phases Zero and One. The requirement in terms of detail is that IT people have to be able to implement the processes in the system based on these descriptions, hence they are implementation guidelines or blueprints. If IT is actively taking part in the project, the detail can possibly be more flexible than if IT did not participate. The process descriptions will be needed for several other purposes too, for instance:

- implementation guideline for IT (as discussed)
- basis for legal quality-control measures (such as the Sarbanes-Oxley Act in the US)
- fulfilment of ISO and other quality guidelines
- working document for future to define measurement points and controls
- working document for future to train personnel and redesign.

Process documentation will always consist of different levels and types of documentation, so it could consist of:

- workflows
- verbal explanations
- executive summary.

One thing is very important to state: there is no way around the detailed process documentation, even if the former processes (in existence somewhere in the organization) are chosen. The time required to carry out the detailed process design can vary but is always a very significant amount of time. One consumer-goods company needed between six and 12 months for a full finance scope in half of Europe. A retail company completed the design for five countries and a full accounting scope in four months. Some companies have been in the design phase basically for years, as they have re-engineered continuously. It can become difficult to see where the phase actually ends. In any case, the design activity is a question of months, maybe years, not of weeks. It is often carried out with substantial resources, internal and external. This is the resource peak in the SSO project.

In the detailed design phase, the scope issues will become more dramatic and there will be fights about the structure of processes. As an example, think about intercompany. This is an area that produces pains for many companies in the form of period-end differences and a large workload to clarify them. In the process design, the first issue will be to define whether intercompany should be a process team of its own or part of some other team. Most companies would choose to have a separate team or to include it in the GA team. Intercompany actually has two different areas:

- the PTP and OTC processes carried out with an internal party – these are similar or should be similar to PTP and OTC
- the remaining difference resolution, which is done in connection with closing activities and hence is often placed into GA.

Greenfield thinking approach

It is important clearly to define who will work on what issues, as the danger is otherwise that two or three teams will all handle intercompany as their topic. The real challenge is to keep clear limits on scope, not forget anything and at the end put the puzzle together again.

In the design phase, project and company management should give advice on the working culture and approach to be used. A consumer-goods company gave the following guidelines for the design work:

- What would a competitor of our size and complexity do if it newly entered Europe?

- Think about best practices and state-of-the-art processes.

- Focus on issues with high improvement potential relative to the required effort/investment.

- Do not feel restricted by today's current structures.

This is a so-called 'greenfield approach' in terms of thinking. It is advisable to move this way, as this thinking process is the only one that opens up potentials previously unknown. A design process based on the existing old platform is a re-engineering approach that cannot deliver quantum-leap results. The greenfield approach needs to be 'made practical' again later, but the generation of ideas should be free in the beginning and then the good ideas should be looked at with the question about whether they actually can be implemented.

Validation

The design is produced by a central project team. To secure the success of this process design team, it is critical to consider the following:

- The design will not be accepted by local sites, if there are only people from HQ in the team. The staffing must be mixed, with all relevant local units represented.

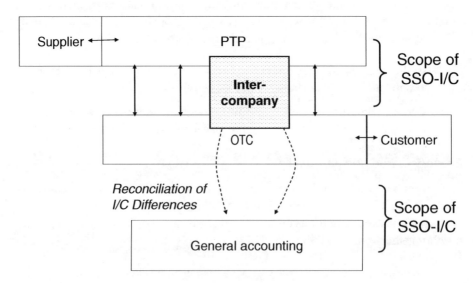

Figure 58   Potential scope of SSO-IC project

- The local entities will not accept the designed results unless explained and discussed. The locals want to give their input and check whether the central team has considered their needs and specifics. The results need to be validated with the local organizations. Therefore, after the first draft is finished, the process teams should go on a validation tour to the different locations and discuss the product. It is useful to have team members from that site present to receive a more favourable reaction.

The validation activity can be performed using centralized workshops, but this will not produce the same benefit. In the local validation approach, local employees will feel better, as the event is 'on their ground'. Also, they have the chance to concentrate on only their issues. In a workshop, everybody will want to explain their specific details, but time will not allow that.

The validation activity will easily take up 30–50% of the design time, so in a six-month design effort there would be two to three months of a road trip for the teams to validate and update the results. The big benefit of this approach is the buy-in received for the implementation. The chances of acceptance are significantly better and this will pay for the effort. The extent of this activity can vary depending on company culture, but some kind of validation should be carried out.

POLICIES AND PROCEDURES

Almost every company has policies and procedures in place. However, most companies are also unhappy with the adherence to these policies and the results they produce (or don't produce). A good example is the intercompany example in Figure 58: most companies have closing guidelines and intercompany guidelines, stating, for instance, that in intra-group activities the receiver of a delivery has to book the internal invoice as it is. Nevertheless, this does not seem to work because the guidelines are not enforced, not adhered to or not working. At period end there is often a difference in the books, or there is a separate list of issues still open.

Policies and procedures for the SSO must be very clear and must work in practice. Otherwise the SSO has no chance to fulfil the service task. They have to be rewritten, based on the new processes. They have to be communicated, trained and enforced. This will take up substantial capacities and produce some pain. Policies and procedures also have to clearly define detailed content, for example:

- account content

- processes to change Chart of Accounts (CoA), P&L, accounts and so on

- detailed limits, such as a materiality limit for dunning

- escalation procedures
- time limits.

The content can be radically bigger or smaller, depending on the SSO structure. In some companies, other departments are responsible for the production guidelines. If this is the case, it is important to team up with these people to introduce them to the SSO idea and necessary changes in processes.

In terms of timing, policies and procedures could be finalized during the implementation phase, but it is useful to work on them after the process design, as this is the time when the process teams have a good overview of the content and can quickly produce useful guidelines.

SYSTEMS AND INFORMATION REQUIREMENTS

When the project set-up is discussed, it is crucial to strive for a combined team structure made up of both finance and IT people. IT people should not be discussion partners or experts; they should be team members and counterparts. This will guarantee the success of the design, as the design will produce processes that actually can be implemented with the available IT platform.

The design suggestions in the process-design activity will be discussed with the IT people and the final process will consider the system ability and requirements. In terms of the deliverables, the workflows will possibly have a separate swim lane for IT, documentation and so on, or the database will have descriptions relevant for the IT implementation. Requirements from an IT point of view – input data, master data and the like – will be considered and built into the process.

The relevance of IT will differ significantly, depending on whether there is a parallel ERP project running. In some cases, such as Henkel and GM, ERP optimization took place in parallel. In such a case the SSO project must strongly coordinate with the IT project. If the ERP go-live date is postponed (which is not uncommon), the SSO project might have to change project planning, perhaps going live without having the new IT platform in place as waiting for it would be even worse.

SSO DESIGN AND GOVERNANCE MODEL

The activities performed here are based on the content described in Part I of this book. Questions that come up in the design phase are discussed below.

Legal entity

The question of whether the SSO should be a separate legal entity can be a tricky one. In the US, this issue would not be considered interesting; in other parts of the world, especially Europe, the legal-entity issue will be significant.

A separate legal entity would bring certain benefits, for example, charging out the services would not only be possible but required. Clear billing mechanisms would be necessary and easier to implement. A different pay scheme might be possible inside this organization. A separate entity is, in many cases, desirable. On the other hand there are issues to solve, such as:

- *Employee representation*: unions and workers' councils could be against a separate entity or require it to take over the same unionized pay and benefit framework agreements in place in other companies. This could result in a bureaucratic and expensive deal. The targeted independence of the SSO could be endangered.

- *Legal representation*: someone will be legally responsible for the entity and such items as health and safety, insurance, local tax and legal contacts.

The ability to set up one SSO entity is also dependent on the current organization structure. It is often necessary to move from several entities per country to one legal entity per country and then in step two to separate certain consolidated services also legally into one entity. The road is difficult due to political and business practice and legal issues, especially tax restrictions. Some companies, like Henkel, had a legal-entity reduction programme run in parallel to the SSO project to support the other in terms of the organization results.

Organization

In terms of other organization alternatives and detailed descriptions, we make reference to Part I of this book. In terms of design steps, it is worth noting that the organization design is not a time-consuming activity but one with significant effects. It has to be decided how far the process thinking will go and the respective organization structure chosen. In reality, the CFO or F&A head often performs an organization design activity as a back-office exercise. This could be the better solution if the company culture is used to top-down rulings. In a democratic culture, the new structure might have to be discussed first. In some cases numerous workshops may be necessary. At some point in the process it is necessary to make clear decisions in terms of individuals not intending to support the new structure. Otherwise they will successfully destroy the SSO before it is finished.

The design activity is best started by defining some organization design principles. This is an example:

- *Customer-focused*: process-based organization structure aligned to customer requirements positions the organization for continuous improvement.

- *Streamlined and flexible organization*: workflows designed for efficient team integration to reduce layers of management and help meet cost-reduction goals.

- *Employee development*: competency building, training and rewards enable high performance and provide skill development and increased growth opportunities.

Governance

Based on content discussed in Part I, the key here is to build a system where reporting lines are clear, escalation paths are clear and decision-making is carried out fast and fruitfully. The governance structure will vary from company to company but it should be built to include a range of roles:

- *Board*: there must be information going up and a framework set top-down.

- *Steering committee*: should be active to support and solve issues without detailed discussions.

- *PMO*: project management office manages the project and its links to other projects.

- *Project management*: possibly included in PMO, the driver to manage SSO content.

- *Project teams*: in general built by process; they do the operative work.

- *Experts from business units*: represent business units and function as contact points.

- *IT*: must be heavily involved in operative and decision-making functions.

- *HR*: must build bridges to employee representatives and legal advisors.

In most cases governance structures are based on hierarchical models, but not necessarily. The project governance structure needs to be in place in parallel with the project organization; the designed governance structure for the SSO operations will be designed during the design phase and possibly completed during implementation.

To finalize the design of the governance model, here are some guiding principles that should be drafted:

- Measure, measure, measure . . . what matters and what's important.

- Set targeted performance levels for each end-to-end process.

- Ensure accountability throughout the end-to-end processes.

- Match the right people to the decisions which are required.

- Back up executive decisions with executive sponsorship for change.

- Leverage SSO/BPO principles to create process savings and improved customer service.

- Support the defined company vision, for instance the improvement in cost management and service levels through end-to-end process redesign.

The decision authority in the governance model must be defined clearly (see Table 52).

Table 52   Decision authority in the governance model

SSO/BPO operating decision	Decision authority		
	SSO/BPO leadership	Customer council	SSO board
Annual operating budget	Submit	Review/challenge	Approve
Annual capital budget	Submit	Review/challenge	Approve
Required capital expenditures (e.g. technology	Submit	Review/challenge	Approve
Significant project commitments	Submit/implement	Review/challenge	Approve
SLA performance levels • financial • process • customer • human capital • organization	Submit/implement	Review/challenge and drive end-to-end-performance improvement	Approve
Process changes across BUs (in-scope processes)	Submit/implement	Review/challenge and drive end-to-end-performance improvement	Approve
Service pricing levels	Submit/implement	Review/challenge	Approve
Fundamental changes in SSC scope – new functions	Submit/implement	Review/challenge	Approve
Additional headcount (within budget)	Submit	Approve	–
Dispute resolution (with BU or corporate)	Initial resolution process	Escalation point	Final disposition

The actual time required from the governance body members differs and the time requirements will diminish once the SSO is established or when the outsourced processes are running smoothly. To aide structuring, all governance activities can be clustered based on necessary time commitment and necessary scope of involvement. Figure 59 is an example to give guidance – though of course, every company must define its own time requirements.

	Focus	Meetings (per quarter)
Exec. board	• Strategic direction • Target setting • Accountability for change	1–3 meetings
Customer council	• Implementing strategy • Business-case development • Operational decisions	6–9 meetings*
SSO/BPO strategic leadership	• Implement strategy • Operational management • Metrics monitoring	Full time

* This time requirement should be cut back to 2–3 days per quarter after improvement initiatives are underway

Figure 59 Time required at governance levels

Naturally the set-up, even the necessity of parts of the governance model, will be a topic of discussion. To perform well in this discussion, it is recommended that the final governance model is prepared with all details before engaging in a broad discussion. Part of this preparation could be the listing of benefits and advantages. In the case of the executive board, the advantage of having one could be questioned and answered by: 'Executive level sponsorship delivers a powerful, strategic advantage to shared services while facilitating culture change and change management.' In detail, the advantages could be:

● End-to-end process cost and quality issues raised to a level where they can be resolved.

● Builds visibility of key performance metrics and improvement opportunities across the company.

● SSO/BPO board can approve targets for the entire end-to-end process in terms of cost and quality levels for the business.

● Creates joint accountability for BU operations and the SSO/BPO provider to meet or exceed targets.

- Ensures investments (for example, budget, capital fund) are in line with strategic directions.

- Supports and bolsters SSO through the change management process.

- Fosters understanding of shared services and outsourcing principles and their strategic advantage throughout the company.

- Allows the SSO/BPO provider to gain valuable knowledge via the expertise of the board's composition.

- Enables strategic relationships and access to key executives and the BUs.

To finalize a successful governance model design, it is also necessary to include:

- roles and responsibilities of all level bodies in detail;

- an executive board charter with definition of cornerstones such as purpose, composition, size, meeting schedule and responsibilities;

- guidance on board staffing, such as characteristics of roles and desired members;

- guidance on customer council staffing, such as a scoring model for voting.

An overview of the roles and responsibilities, based on a US company example, could include:

- Executive board:
  - executive sponsorship
  - strategic focus
  - facilitates organizational buy-in
  - operating and capital budget approval.

- Customer council:
  - change agent/partner, with shared services, to sponsor improvement initiatives across the BUs and the overall company
  - identifies and secures ad-hoc resources to design and implement improvements
  - assesses and resolves issues which cross organizational lines
  - develops cases for action for the executive board

- SSO strategic leadership:
  - builds partnerships across BUs and the overall company
  - manages shared services activities through SLAs
  - accountable for delivery of financial, process, customer, human capital and organizational objectives/targets.

- Process leaders (team leaders):
  - align processes with shared services goals
  - determine how to fulfil customer service requirements
  - manage process-based activities
  - execute training and development activities.

Ultimately the governance model needs broad acceptance to have a chance to function.

DESIGN SLAs AND PERFORMANCE MEASURES

We discussed the necessity of SLAs, SLA content and metrics in Chapters 6 and 7. In terms of design work on this content, some of the learnings from past projects include:

Timing

Most companies nowadays start designing SLAs before they even know what the processes in the SSO will look like. Clearly, this is not useful. The timing of activities should follow the necessity of doing something, not the ability or interest of individuals. In terms of the SLA, it should only be drafted after there is an agreed-upon process split between local and central and the service scope has been discussed. The SLA can be drafted in the design phase, but often there will be finalization work on it necessary during implementation. Naturally it is useful to have an SLA in place when service provision begins, but in reality SLAs are often designed and agreed upon when services are already underway.

Content

The content discussion is difficult and should be well prepared by the SSO project teams. The main question, often jumped over, is simple: 'What do we need the SLA for?' As stupid as this might seem, it is critical. The SLA can be necessary as:

- a contractual document

- a legal document

- a scope definition document

- a performance measurement platform

- a change management tool

- or a combination of all these purposes.

The design can only take place after clear agreement on the purpose. The content will then meet the purpose of the SLA and the depth of the SLA will be governed by this.

The design itself should be carried out by a small specialized team. These people should have benchmarking experience and process knowledge. They then should propose:

- a set of KPIs

- the automation solution for getting the KPIs (in detail)

- the SLA text

and discuss with project management. A final draft then needs to be discussed with the clients. Often small individual changes per client are necessary. As the SLA is also a change management tool, it is helpful to agree to these changes and standardize later. The SLA has a life-cycle of its own, anyway, and will be changed probably after one year of operations.

In geographical areas with tight regulatory environments, the SLA tends to become a legal document used to convince authorities of a legally acceptable approach and organizational set-up:

- In Germany, the SLA is often necessary as a piece of a documentation chain to convince tax authorities about the exact content of the SSO work. This is based on the tax issues around the German Tax Act (GTA) legislation which prohibits the move of accounting decision-making abroad.

- In China it is only allowed for an employee to provide work output (services in the SSO) to his or her actual employer, not to another entity. That would mean that the employees of the SSO need to have employment contracts with their customers, who then are not customers any more but employers. Also, the different licences that the entities operating in China hold are relevant in terms of tasks that they are allowed to perform. Keeping with such requirements is a difficult task and the resulting SLAs obviously have very different functionalities.

KPI model

The basis for the measurement is a KPI model. The benchmarking definitions and scope from the feasibility phase can be used as a platform, but often the company has its own steering ideas and certain specific measurements required but not available in external benchmarking models. Also, there are industry-specific KPIs that should be considered. All these inputs need to be built into a hypothesis model which is then tested and finally updated and finalized. This KPI model needs to be communicated to both the performing personnel as well as the ones to be measured (see Figure 60).

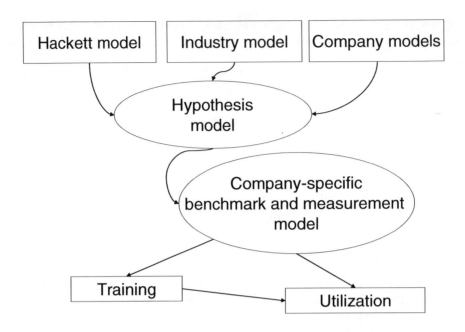

Figure 60   Set-up of individual KPI model

The set of KPIs resulting from such a KPI model is a good basis for the KPI list in an attachment to an SLA. This now makes it obvious why a first-draft SLA might have to be used with a selection of useful KPIs, before such a KPI model work package has been concluded and the 'final' set is delivered.

All measurements – and with them the contractual documents defining their use – are worthless, if they are not linked to:

- overall targets by scorecards and so on
- individual performance by individual targets in annual performance interviews or contracts
- training plans
- individual pay in the variable salary components.

World-class companies pay bonuses more frequently to reward the highest levels of productivity and quality. A visible outcome of a linkage of strategy and action and of a commitment to performance measurement is the fact that world-class companies paid spot bonuses for positive performance on change projects in 78% of cases (59% more than average companies).

In the example of a consumer-goods company, the discussion about the linkage of SSO project performance with pay took several months (in the middle of the design phase). At the end, two results were achieved:

- The award-system basis was not changed. The culture of the company required awards to have positive effect and the way the rewards were implemented was that basically everybody received 100% of the bonus, the 'really good' performance then resulted in overachievement and 100+%. It was not possible to tie the 100% bonus, for example, to a full achievement of the SSO timetable. This was considered too radical and culturally unacceptable.

- The bonus content, however, was linked to the SSO project – in some cases with a significant portion, although only specified by a percentage. The individual targets would have included points such as successful management of an SSO team or successful change management or provision of best-practice designs for processes in scope. The targets did not specify what 'successful' meant, but the benefit of this was a lean target definition and discussion process and the recipients still got the message in terms of the importance of bringing the project to a successful end.

HR TRANSITION PLAN

No SSO project is based on the target of personnel reduction. People who tell you that SSO is a cost-cutting exercise have either not understood the concept or are simply using a progressive and popular name for their own initiative on something else. Nevertheless, since cost savings are a standard goal in any SSO implementation, the results will in most cases include effects on people in the negative sense too: redundancy and outplacement.

The business case set up during the feasibility phase will include a fairly good assessment of the effects on personnel, at least as an overall number and in terms of financials. It does not include a detailed list of persons by name. This, however, will be the case after the design is completed. All employees in scope can be assessed based on the consolidation and process-activity transfer results. It is a simple task to calculate how many roles are needed in future locally, how many centrally and how many are redundant. HR has to be involved here, as well as line managers, to then put names behind the numbers. This will be a tricky task because of all the criteria to be considered. These criteria can also vary significantly in terms of countries. The result will be:

- a matrix with all personnel movements
- an HR transition plan with times and activities.

Depending on the exact project status, there will normally be three groups of employees:

- those who should be kept
- those necessary for the remainder of the project
- those who are or will become redundant.

The first two groups urgently need individual discussions. Their employment should be secured, permanently or for the time period required. Group 3 should be treated fairly and receive the truth as soon as possible to give them clarity and a fair chance to find other jobs. Some companies offer outplacement support. The HR transition plan needs to link with the implementation plan and the best way through this difficult process is the straight truth.

PILOTS

The implementation plan will detail a timetable for the entities and countries in terms of their roll-in. It is useful to time the countries based on the following rules:

- Start with something small and easy, to secure a quick win and keep momentum going.
- Ask for volunteers – normally there are some.
- Have large countries follow soon to move volumes to SSO quickly in order to get the calculated benefits.
- Move difficult countries (those with political issues, legal problems or high resistance) to the end of the timetable.
- In some cases, countries with high resistance need to be migrated fast, especially if they spread their resistance (if they voice it actively and demoralize the rest).

The first small countries or entities can be considered pilots. They are test cases and receive more support than others will receive later. Therefore it might be useful to be a pilot. The pilots will never be let down – they will always succeed, as it is important to show success in the beginning. It is similar to being one of the pilot users for new software. The vendor cannot allow you to dislike the product and will solve the bugs fast to secure ultimate satisfaction. The SSO pilots are sometimes carried out during or at the end of the design phase; sometimes they are just the first ones in the implementation timetable and hence in the implementation phase. That is not relevant since design and implementation link up very closely. The importance lies in the definition of an implementation plan that includes pilots, where certain implementation steps can be 'tested'.

MANAGE PROGRAMME AND PROJECT AND ENABLE CHANGE

Every project has some key success criteria, and one of them is always a good project manager. Especially in SSO projects, both the internal actively and operationally responsible managers and the active internal and external coaches are of extreme importance. The team is important too, but definitely a successful project depends on a good project manager and the best team cannot succeed without a good manager. A good project manager needs at least three things:

- a strong will to succeed

- experience in performing such a role

- a good tool kit to implement the ideas with success.

Do spend time to find the right people to run your project. The wrong decisions here will help neither yourself nor the chosen ones.

Every project is run by a project manager, but in some cases the projects are too big to be handled by only one person. In this case it makes sense to install a programme manager. The programme manager manages a programme consisting of several projects and subprojects. The programme manager (or the organizational box he or she fulfils) is sometimes also called programme management office (PMO). The PMO does not get involved in the details of the projects. It plans all work streams, resources and activities and controls the result delivery and time-lines. The PMO is the planning and controlling unit of a project. The important decision is about the size of the total project and the necessity for a two-level management structure (under a steering committee). On a simple geographically and FTE-wise limited project a PMO will not be necessary. It becomes necessary when FTEs, BUs and entities increase in number. It definitely is vital when an SSO project is cross-continental or runs in connection with an ERP project or similar.

The PMO will work mainly based on one huge planning document, often set up as a programme evaluation and review technique (PERT) chart using software such as MS Project or similar tools. The PMO will discuss with the steering committee and the project managers and try to match the two views. The PMO also has the role of actively pushing the project managers and teams to reach the defined goals. In this role PMO is 'the long arm of the steering committee'. There are numerous things to consider in terms of how to run a project – they could fill a whole book on project management. Here, we will just mention some experiences from SSO projects as guidance:

- The key to a successful SSO project is good preparation; this needs to consider:
  - *staffing*: recruit good people or at least find a reasonable compromise between excellent players and the 'available ones'
  - *resources*: do not use 20% resources – participation levels below 50% are useless. The update of these people takes up the available time
  - *budget*: include 20–30% security buffer for unplanned adjustments. This is 'air' at the time of planning but will most certainly be necessary even if the project runs well.

- Secure visible top-management support: ensure it is not only 'existing' but also 'visible'. Top management must participate in selected meetings and clearly push messages into the organization about the importance of SSO.

- Find a good balance between checking the validity of ideas and pushing forward. Good measurements for speed are the acceptance of results reported upwards combined with satisfaction of team members in the project.

- Be bold in trusting ideas that make sense – do not simply copy things that have been implemented at least ten times.

- Remember that the SSO project is primarily a change management effort, not a technological or organizational issue.

The change management issues cannot be stressed often enough because experience shows that even in the most understanding and acquiescent environments there is normally no ability or willingness actually to spend money on the change process, even though the change necessity is agreed by everyone to be priority number one. This might have to do with the fact that management often believes change issues to be soft issues that are uncomfortable for the employees but do not really affect the process or performance. Now this is clearly not the case. The pitfalls of an SSO project in terms of change management topics lie not only in motivational areas. There are also operational issues, sometimes resulting from motivational neglect.

Change management pitfalls in a SSO project due to motivational issues include:

- best people leave

- performance decreases

- people block new processes

- people refuse to learn new abilities

- people play CFO, PO and project lead against each other.

The operational issues include:

- best-practice know-how leaves with key personnel
- variations occur in actually implemented processes
- design and implementation phase consumes much more time than calculated
- there is a quality slump due to overwork
- there is a sub-optimal performance due to a lack of information.

The example bulleted above, from a company's design phase change issues, clearly shows the motivational and operational fears – some of them materialized and have not been solved until today. Reading through clever research about change enablers, it is striking how similar the results are: it is always the 'voting with feet' by employees as protest or unwillingness to support change that makes projects fail. Still, projects are often triggered as if nobody ever learnt anything about this topic and any target could be achieved by implementing the Prussian Order Book.

The culture and behaviours of the design phase will be taken over to the next phases. Teams often stay unchanged. Errors here will remain errors in the future phases.

CHAPTER 12

Implementation

ESTABLISHING THE SSO

The design and implementation phases will always run slightly in parallel. The first entities or countries being rolled in could be in implementation, while certain process details or organizational alignments are still being designed (or at least discussed and decided). Also, implementation will run in parallel with optimization. All countries rolled into the SSO are, by definition, after their 'go-live' in optimization. Other countries are still to be incorporated and hence are in the design or implementation stages. The phasing therefore only holds true per entity or country, not for everybody at the same time.

The big difference between design and implementation is the fact that the structures designed are now being used operationally. That means that:

- processes now are done differently
- activities are performed by different people and in different places
- a different IT support is being utilized.

For those units and people that are rolled into the SSO, this is a major change and the start of the future. The rolling-in of activities and persons is the main part of actually establishing the SSO. The other side of the establishment are contracts, personnel decisions and so on, but the 'real thing' is the physical SSC with physical people, actual operations and solutions performed the new way.

The principal target of project management and operations management is now to 'keep things rolling'. The SSO needs to be made known and 'sold' as quickly as possible to be sure of its future. Volume is important but so is quality and client satisfaction. In many cases, operations are ahead of contractual activities, and they need to be as they cannot stand still for days or weeks because of budget discussions.

SITE SELECTION AND BUILD-UP

Before the operations started, there must have been a site selection and build-up. The site is selected as the last step of the location and site-assessment process that started in the feasibility phase. The actual building and the space in which personnel will work are the most important things to those actually working in that SSC. There will be a different set of criteria necessary to evaluate the working space, criteria such as:

- motivational aspects

- team support of space usage

- ergonomic aspects (such as comfortable chairs and screens)

- legal, health and safety aspects: keeping within regulations and possibly doing a bit more

- logistics to and from the SSC: is there a bus route or are there support measures for certain employees necessary to get them to the site?

- food: where it can be bought, prepared and consumed.

Food is not considered a big issue but in an international SSC employees could have different eating habits and even religious requirements over how and what to eat. It could be necessary to provide space for the preparation of certain meals. Issues such as prayer breaks for the religious or the possibility to wear specific clothing must be solved upfront. In some European countries there is an ongoing legal and cultural dispute about, for instance, whether Muslim clothing is allowed in the work environment. This might be a limiting factor for the location choice or later on in terms of employee selection.

Industrialized countries especially have a range of legislation in place explaining in detail what a chair should be like and what computer screens must do or not do (for example, in terms of radiation). There is a list of insurance issues to solve and most of these things will be controlled by a public authority. It is useful to have a site manager role filled during the site build-up and afterwards in operations.

BUILD IT INFRASTRUCTURE

The IT infrastructure is very important and can also be very costly. The build-up will have to be coordinated with the implementation schedule and the site preparation activities. The original assumptions about the IT cost need to be verified as the business case does not know the site specifics yet, so the amount of building work necessary (new cables, sockets and so on) could differ significantly from the original assumptions. The changes to the buildings have to be discussed with the landlord of the space. In some cases the leaseholder may do the changes as part of the rent agreement. The IT infrastructure set-up must be coordinated then with the preparation work so it matches time-wise.

Another issue will be the choice between the purchase of new IT equipment or the transport of existing equipment to the SSC. This must be decided individually – no general rule applies here. The trend is to outsource everything connected to expensive equipment, like scanning, so it might be sufficient to use the old scanners if the local outsourcing step will take place later on. However, technical capabilities need to match.

RISK IDENTIFICATION AND RISK MITIGATION

The original risk identification and mitigation plan needs to be updated during implementation. It is very important to track the issues and document them. This will require substantial efforts as the amount of issues and solutions will be huge. Tracking, however, is the only realistic chance to really solve the problems. The approach of 'quick decisions and trust in the employee' will not work, because there are too many interdependences between issues and the employee structure will change constantly in SSO operations.

The most important effect to follow here is the hockey-stick effect, explained in Chapter 3 of this book. The performance will fall initially before it gets better and costs and resources will increase initially before any benefits kick in. The close measurement and management of the hockey-stick effect is the main management task in this phase. The hockey stick will not take up this form automatically. Only a range of measures used effectively will actually improve the situation and lead the company out of this 'valley of despair'. Without action, the SSO would not be successful.

TRAIN STAFF

The training activities must start before the SSO is in its implementation phase. IT-related aspects in particular need to be trained before operations start. Nevertheless, a successful SSO will need to have a good training programme in place. The basic idea is to split work packages in such a way that new employees can be trained to work on them very fast. The higher fluctuation in the SSO environment will lead to the actual necessity to perform the training measures more often than in other organizations. The training must be in the form of well-prepared ready packages that can be taken from the shelf when fluctuation or growth kicks in.

In some circumstances, additional training measures are necessary. As Japan Tobacco International (JTI) entered the Manchester SSO market, other SSCs in the area, including Marks & Spencer and Michelin, were unhappy because JTI attracted some of their employees by paying higher salaries. They could not raise their own pay too much, so other measures became necessary. They included in their job packages courses at local universities or language courses, for instance in French. Training measures are a preparation for the job but also part of the remuneration package and hence an important component in general.

Work shadowing

The best training activity is work shadowing. When taking over local activities, it is critical to move knowledge from the old employees to the new SSC employees. The old employees will have a lot of special knowledge that is not documented. They will know specifics about customer and vendor history, past compromises, system issues, tips and tricks. This know-how must be secured, as that is the value-adding piece in the performance. The only way this can work is by asking the old employee to explain these things to another new colleague. Basically the new colleague will sit next to the experienced person and watch that person work through a set of activities. The new employee will ask questions, make notes and ultimately understand the processes and memorize tricks and specifics not documented so far.

The difficulty in performing this activity is of course the fact that the former employee will know the reasons for this activity. It is basically impossible to hide the true reasons. Hence, the former employee will know that he or she is actually asked to train his or her successor. Nobody will find this an attractive task – most people would refuse. It is therefore important to make the reasons transparent and be open and honest about the whole exercise. Another necessary step is to discuss the future career options for that 'old' employee and offer an incentive, for example, a bonus. It is not uncommon to pay 50–100% of an annual salary for a former employee as a 'training bonus' in such cases. The former employees will in most cases (probably as high as 90%) actually agree to doing this. The reasons are:

- they can no longer change their future career options
- they will be interested in the financial compensation
- they will think that things might change during the next one or two years so they might still have a chance
- they might accept the work-shadowing period as a well-paid search time to look for other jobs
- they will be happy about the fact that somebody is finally interested in what they actually do – this is something accounting employees are normally not asked but will be happy to explain.

The work-shadowing activities have to be well planned. They require both the former and new employees to be at the specific training site (the old local operations) at planned times. The length of such a training can be between one week and two months per process area, depending on the complexity. Usually the work-shadowing block will be for a duration of two to four months. Managing the work shadowing can be very stressful. Employees will report in ill, even if they agreed to the bonus. Legally there are often no measures against this. Employees will perform the work shadowing but will not do their utmost to remember all possible tricks. This cannot be controlled.

In summary, there are many reasons why the transfer of activities to the new SSC should be carried out in such a way that some of the former local employees are still available for problem solving after the SSC is up and running. They will (in most cases) be interested in travelling to the SSC to help, and sometimes even change their mind after seeing the operations.

FINALIZE SLAs

As mentioned under the design phase, the SLAs will be a living document and will probably be changed again here in the implementation phase. It is useful to change performance measurements in the SLA after practical operations have delivered first results.

ROLL-OUT

There will be a roll-out or roll-in plan for the implementation phase. The wording depends on what is being done or described:

- the processes are mostly rolled out to all entities
- a new system is rolled out throughout the company to be used by everybody
- the activities that can be performed centrally are rolled in (into the SSC)
- the FTE that migrate to the SSC site are being rolled into the SSC.

Such a roll-out plan will detail the order of things to come, an example being Figure 61.

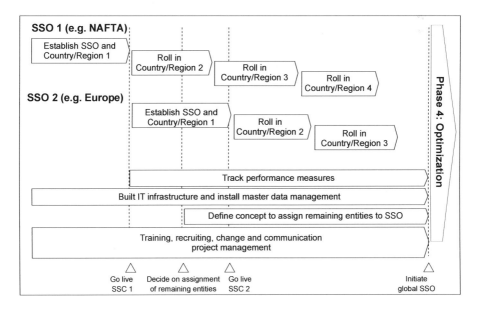

Figure 61   Outline project plan for Phase Three: implementation and deployment

Every implementation schedule will look a little different and often needs to be adapted during implementation several times.

SYSTEM INTEGRITY

Issues linked to the design, but not finalized during design, will be on the agenda during implementation. Especially in the case of linkage between SSO and ERP project activities (but also in other cases) it will be necessary to cover all issues that have to do with system integrity:

- authorization concept
- training of employees
- defined processes
- system security
- data distribution and interfaces
- split of responsibility.

Most of these activities will be carried out by the IT colleagues. Some of them are of high relevance for the SSO people, one of these being the authorization concept. The ERP system (for instance, SAP) has a specified system of describing and organizing who can perform what activities and who can access what areas of the system and data. This needs to be designed and organized. However, the design of the authorization concept can only be performed after the process design has finished. The authorization concept will be built on defined roles and usage rights connected to these roles. To define the roles, it must be clear what activities in the new processes must be performed by whom, what roles are necessary.

This 'design'-related activity should run before operational activities can be performed. It often does not. Employees will then work based on existing roles and the old authorization concept. This can be done for some time but complicates processes and adds risk. The design of the authorization concept itself can be a substantial amount of work and take several FTEs several months to complete.

MASTER DATA

One of the most labour-intensive work packages underestimated most often is the master data work stream. It is often 'forgotten' that the SSO will need more than a process, people and a system. The system will need data to work on. This data can be split into two main categories:

- master data
- input data.

Master data build the working basis and include such data as:

- account numbers in Chart of Accounts (CoA)
- cost elements for controlling
- customer numbers
- vendor numbers.

The master data need to be defined, because the SSO is based on standard processes and often a standard system. The data formats have to fit into this set-up, so, for example, there can only be one CoA with one defined structure, eight-digit account numbers instead of six digits.

It can be quite difficult to define what master data are precisely. ERP systems will deliver a basic definition, but still there can be a lot of discussion as to whether these elements are master data around such areas as:

- profit-centre groups
- exchange rates
- internal orders.

In terms of scope, it is also necessary to define what master data design and (later) management should include. Is it just the format definition or also such areas as:

- SAP scripts
- standard reports
- customizing data?

The master-data activities in order are:

- data identification and structuring
- data format design
- data harmonization
- maintenance process design and implementation
- quality assurance.

After consideration of all issues, the scope can be defined for:

- master-data design

- structure of possible organizational unit controlling master-data issues, for example a centre of expertise.

The master-data activity can be extremely large. In an example of a European SSO implementation, the master data stream took almost one year and for at least half a year provided work for between three and five persons (internal plus external). The extent of the master-data work is naturally very much dependent on the status quo at the time of starting but, even with a standardized system landscape, some master-data validation work will be necessary.

HEALTH CHECK

The SSO project will take several years and many employees will get tired or frustrated about their job or the project progress. In some cases, there might be intrapersonal problems that slow down the progress. In any project running this long, it is helpful to check the 'health of the project' at certain intervals, perhaps after every one or two years. A good test is the health check, when an independent and external party will carry out a small research. The project members are given the chance to voice their opinions about the project on an anonymous basis. This questionnaire will include information about:

- project progress

- their role

- their overall satisfaction

- issues with project management

- issues with colleagues

- internal team problems

- critical expectations and things that have to change.

This health check will have to be carried out by external and neutral persons. A consultant not involved in the project can receive the answers by e-mail and put together a report. The results are then presented to the project team including the respondents as well as the project management. The team then needs to work out a list of measures to solve the issues that come up. It is not allowed for team leaders to know who answered what or to disagree with the results.

In sum the health check should help project members to voice their worries without risking their careers. The most important reaction must be action – no action would make the exercise useless, even counter-productive.

CHAPTER 13

Optimization

PROCESS STABILIZATION

The number one priority in implementation and in optimization is the so-called process of stabilization. This means that the newly implemented processes or process changes often produce some problems in the beginning (in terms of the hockey-stick effect) and need some time to start to run smoothly. The stabilization activities are not a few specific ones but the full list of all measures necessary to make the processes run stably and successfully. The process stabilization is actually implementation work carried over to the next phase because of implementation and performance problems. The implementation really ends when the process runs stably.

PERFORMANCE EVALUATION

Whether or not the implementation and stabilization have been successful can only be determined if measured. All performance measurement and evaluation tools mentioned before become extremely important again in the optimization phase. Often, there has been no time to really evaluate performance and set up measurements before. When the SSO has finally reached its operational phase, the project teams convert to operational teams and the measurements are not just a question of project success but of operational delivery. Therefore, the measurements need to be constant. Performance evaluation becomes a fact of operational SSO life.

When playing around with numbers, it is useful to also try to understand where the improvements are actually coming from (see Table 53).

In the implementation of an SSO, benefits come from three 'baskets':

- standardization
- consolidation
- re-engineering.

Consolidation and standardization in most cases count for about two thirds to three quarters of the total achievable benefit. Re-engineering will deliver the rest. If a company has implemented all the best practices for process improvements that are available, the next 10% of improvements will obviously not come from that corner. If a

Table 53   Sources of savings for shared service centres

	Saving potential (% of total savings)
Re-engineer	
● Leverage technology	25
● Optimize practices, process flows, organization and policies	
● 'Customized' organization	
● Adopt internal 'best operating practices'	
Standardize	
● Standardize policies and processes	25–50
● Minimize number of systems	
Consolidate	
● Reduce physical locations	25–50
● Consolidate organization and streamline	
● Opportunistic standardization	

company has one pan-European SSC in place then consolidation will not deliver anything any more – re-engineering or a location change might. It is critical to understand the numbers and what can and what cannot be done with the available tools. Therefore, detailed performance evaluations are useful to exhibit what tools work and when they stop working.

SSO DEVELOPMENT

The up-and-running SSO will need to be optimized and improved constantly. Continuous improvement and re-engineering will be necessary. The SSO will possibly change and be developed further. Options here include, for example:

- *Expand:* SSOs are often expanded during their operations in terms of:
  - additional processes
  - additional countries
  - additional entities
  - additional content
  - additional responsibility.
- *Outsource:* the SSO could over time be outsourced partly or wholly.
- *Virtualize:* the SSO could convert into a virtual network.

- *Commercialize:* the SSO could sell its services to a external party and become a BPO.

The future developments of a specific SSO are difficult to predict as the future of SSOs in general is unforeseeable. Most companies worry little about the future trends in SSO, but concentrate on improving the SSO's performance and becoming world-class or best practice.

WORLD-CLASS FINANCE ORGANIZATION

The most difficult question is: What is a world-class finance organization? In this book we have displayed best practices, improvement ideas, metrics and so forth. Still, a world-class organization could be described in many ways. According to Hackett it could be the top 10% of performers in terms of value and efficiency. Others choose different definitions.

In reality, the target setting and the implementation of the suite of measures to get there (or at least closer to there) are important, not the definitions. The following is an example of a consumer-goods company.

The starting situation of this company in its support areas until 1999 was:

- it had carried out 50+ administrative projects

- 80% of projects failed

- decentralized 'kingdoms' existed for everything

- there was no transparency

- there was no control

- it suffered from high costs

- it achieved low quality

- there were no synergies from mergers and acquisitions

- it had a heterogeneous IT

- many employees had an unmotivated mind-set.

In order to become 'world-class' the company defined a target in terms of benchmarking baseline and a programme of measures which they carried out over the following years, as presented in Figure 62.

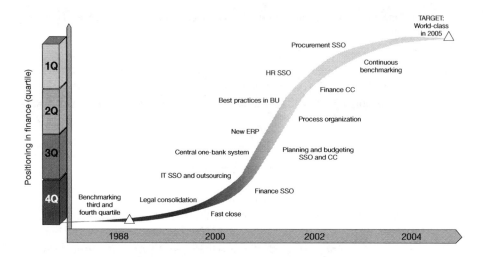

Figure 62   Road map from benchmarking to world-class finance

This road map from benchmarking to world-class in Figure 62 includes several projects within finance but also projects in areas such as procurement, which will have an effect on finance. The SSO is only one component within this improvement programme. It is important to remember that although the excitement for an SSO can become blinding for those inside the SSO, the true goal is not the SSO itself. Strategically, the SSO is also just a tool in a larger suite of measures.

To fulfil its role inside finance to reach world-class, it is (for us finance people) interesting to know how the world-class targets for the finance function can be described. If we compile Hackett research, the world-class profile could be:

- A world-class finance organization is not just about cost, it is synonymous with well-managed and controlled business.

- A world-class finance organization utilizes best practices in all areas:
  - planning and reporting is faster, simpler and more reliable
  - risk management provides security by routinely minimizing risk
  - processes are automated, error-free and lean
  - organization is based on and attracts pools of experts (competence centres and SSO)
  - people are a motivated and talented corps of finance specialists
  - technology is truly and passionately used to standardize and reduce complexity.

- A world-class finance organization constantly strives to improve itself in order to serve the company – even if that would mean dismantling itself.

Inside the SSO optimization phase, the main orientation points for the SSO should be the company targets and the support to fulfil them and to optimize in this direction. As can be seen in the above example, a major activity is the linkage of the SSO project with other company initiatives and their timing within the total improvement programme.

Future Trends

Some say there will be only two types of companies in the future: those who outsource and those who do outsourcing. Others feel that all manual work will disappear in the course of automation and only a small portion of exception handling will remain. Yet others think that virtual atomic corporations of the future will work in unconsolidated network structures. Certainly, the best way to predict the future is to invent it, but for those who prefer a more reactive approach, the future of shared services is a riddle and everybody is invited to help solve it.

TRENDS IN SSO

Trends in the SSO arena have been quite similar and consistent for years, even across geographies. Between the US and Europe, weighting and speed of developments do differ but the broad trends in terms of future development direction are similar:

- Most multinationals have already moved to a global SSO concept made up of between three and five regional SSCs (e.g. pan-European SSC).

- Smaller companies are currently on the move from local sites to national SSCs.

- Organizations with some years of SSO experience constantly increase number of countries and processes supported from a single SSC.

- Shared services are successfully being implemented across all industries supporting the view of their content being classified as non-core.

- Companies tend to use the phased approach more often (that is, moving stepwise from several locations to a few locations and then to one SSC).

- Technology keeps improving and is increasingly enabling companies to consider more and more opportunities.

- The SSO broadens to cover more than just the finance function (procurement, customer services, HR, IT, for instance) and becomes an integrated business centre.

- Companies with SSO experience move up the value chain resulting in scope changing to exceptions handling and these SSCs increasingly housing more value-adding people.

- There is an increasing trend towards outsourcing parts of or complete SSOs.

- There is growing consideration of virtual solutions.

Peter Drucker said that 'The best way to predict the future is to invent it'. In SSOs that definitely holds true and the big excitement is around the fact that there is still time for everybody to take a guess about future developments. The best companies will want neither to just wait for developments nor to put all their eggs in one basket. Nevertheless, for world-class companies and those who just want to survive, it is necessary to be fast. Wayne Gretsky put it this way: 'The good player skates to where the puck is, the great player skates to where the puck is going to be.' Based on current trends, the outlook could be:

- SSCs will keep moving up the value chain and increasingly house more value-adding people:
  - dealing with exceptions
  - performing planning and control activities
  - performing business analysis
  - providing technology support.

- SSCs, especially for lower-value work, will increasingly be located in lower labour cost countries (Eastern Europe, India).

- There will be three or more tiers of SSCs inside the SSO: global, regional, local/country and an outsourced back-up solution.

- There will be more outsourcing in general and increased usage of industry and ASP solutions.

- SSCs will be used as standardized hubs for e-business initiatives.

- SSOs will expand their functionality beyond finance to include procurement, HR, IT, marketing, customer services and so on.

It seems to be that even though the trends and the outlook provide direction and a set of alternatives, there seem to be three main routes to choose from, as displayed in Figure 64.

In past development, companies originally used to operate in diverse and decentralized environments. Then the wave of organizing by internal centres (cost centre, profit centre and so on) brought a change in the thinking, as suddenly the total benefit was not perceived to be the sum of full independence for everybody but instead as the centrally organized provision of standardized work output. The third step was to question why every entity would need its centre structure – why not the group in total? If

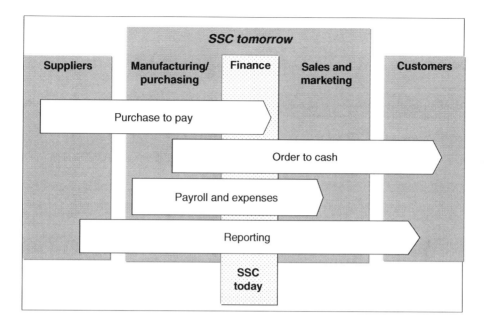

Figure 63   Deepening scope of SSC

we have 200 entities with, say, 50 accounting departments organized as centres, why not have only one? Where would the optimal number be between one and 200? Currently most companies are in the big bubble in the middle, looking at an SSO solution or having a national or regional SSO solution in place. In terms of future direction, the question is: what happens after the national/regional consolidation effort?

There is no doubt about the fact that many SSO will keep optimizing their processes and some of them will reach a state close to 'lights-out processing' where only exception handling is necessary. In this case, the work content will change from transactional to a more competence-centre type of work and staffing will have to change to more skilled personnel. Although the wage differential between alternative sites will still be interesting, the availability of this workforce is more restricted than for transactional personnel and hence location alternatives will be fewer.

In general, the different alternatives companies will have are:

- *Automate:* move work into the machine.

- *Relocate:* move work to cheaper location.

- *Self-service:* move work to another stakeholder (employee, customer, vendor).

- *Outsource:* move work to an external party.

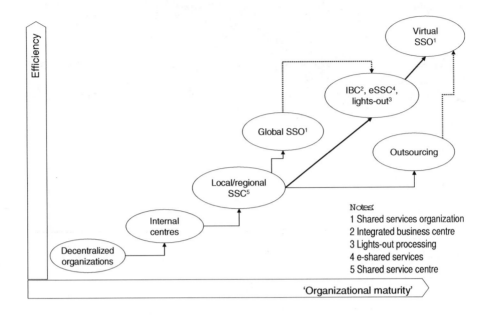

Figure 64   Development of shared services

Considering self-service to be a variation of automation (otherwise it would just be a different work split in the value chain) and hence just a tool, we are left with three structural directions to choose from:

- *Global SSO:* move to a global SSO solution with few centres in low-cost locations.

- *Outsourcing:* move the execution to an outside party who is specialized in providing this type of support.

- *Integrated business centre (IBC):* move work into the machine by automating, by installing best practices and by leveraging technology.

Faced with the above alternatives, most companies initially choose not to want to outsource and not to want to move to another location. It is initially much more appealing to choose the IBC alternative, because this way it looks possible to keep the current structure, locations and most of the people. The problem is the following:

- The IBC solution requires high investment in technology and process improvements whereas the other two alternatives can be realized with little investment and in a shorter time frame.

- The IBC solution will require that FTEs are also reduced in scope, just not by geographical move but by redundancy because of process optimization.

Ultimately, the IBC solution will also lead to a state with fewer FTEs in a modern, automated, best-practice environment. This environment will have to be service-oriented, so it will be an SSC – not a back office. The only difference is really that the IBC route will enable the project responsibles to reduce FTEs by different tools also ending at an FTE figure so low that the discussion stops because of lack of volume. This volume will, presumably, not be far away from the volumes considered necessary or useful for the SSO storyline. Hence, the result will be:

- all routes will lead to a service environment

- all support functions of the future will be organized as SSOs

- all directions possible will eventually lead to FTE reduction to a non-material level

- the real decision is on investment, not on target.

In terms of trying to answer the questions most frequently asked about the SSO future, the result could also be:

- Shared services are here to stay – for as long as necessary until outsourcing takes over. 'The question is not whether to outsource but when to outsource.'

- 'You have to breathe in to be able to breathe out', in other words, set up an SSO to be able to standardize and then (possibly) get rid of it (compare also virtual SSO below).

- All the above trends are part of our reality. 'The choice is not to buy a ticket for a train or not to buy it – the choice is to pick one of the trains that are leaving, or to be left at the station.'

All the above discussion is based (in general) on the scope of transactional processes. The complication of such an assessment is that the line between processes suitable for transactional SSO and for competence centres is on the move. Much of the discussion in the future will therefore be less about the validity of the above trends and scenarios and more about the lines to be drawn between central and local.

OUTSOURCING VERSUS INTERNAL SSO

We have covered this comparison of outsourcing versus internal SSO in detail in Chapter 10. It is a decision strongly related to the future outlook considerations of any company. Companies that do reach something like a 'market level' in the provision of their services will be faced with the decision to possibly commercialize, to sell their services to external providers (become an outsourcer). Some will undoubtedly do that, but the outsourcing market will presumably only support a handful of large operators (plus local niche players), so opportunities are getting fewer. The market is today so mature that advice to become a BPO cannot be given.

The question about complete outsourcing instead of setting up shared services does not seem to be the correct question, since outsourcing really does seem to be the next development step after the SSO, at least for everybody able to set up their own SSO first. The question is, rather, whether a corporation is mature enough to perform a quantum leap and jump directly to outsourcing or, on the contrary, the entity feels it is not capable of performing the 'cleaning up' of its back office itself. The 'cleaning-up' service has a price tag, so the logical path is to clean up first by using the tool of SSO and then to outsource with clearly defined processes, tasks, responsibilities and so on. Based on current trends, BPOs are growing and it remains to be seen where their growth will stop. So far there is no limitation in sight yet.

VIRTUAL SHARED SERVICES

Virtual shared services seems to be an electrifying topic. People have been seen to travel thousands of kilometres to a conference to listen only to this one presentation and then go back home. It might be the 'last bastion of hope' for those who are and strictly will remain against SSOs. And they do have some criteria in their favour.

According to organization theory, the ultimate organizational solution is a virtual network that consists of atomic elements working seamlessly together. It is necessary to point out that this view exists and that it provides one definition for virtual shared services. We also used this as a basis in the above discussion about trends.

Our interest here is more in the short- and medium-term solutions and a different definition of virtual shared services. As no company is even close to the above state, it does help more to take this approach: until anybody can reach this optimal future state, the question is whether the consolidation element in the SSO is so important that it must be implemented or whether 'virtual' SSOs yield similar benefits with less hassle.

This question is valid because of the logical review of arguments generally used in favour of SSOs. We could question the consolidation necessity based on the use of the following enablers:

- Web-enabled self-service applications *enable* data entry and query resolution to be pushed to suppliers, customers and employees.

- Standardized and integrated ERP systems (for example, a single global instance) *enable* the minimizing of rekeying of data within the organization and allow common global process models to be implemented and to work.

- The increased use of OCR, scanning, workflow as well as increased use of business-to-business integration through EDI, XML and other standards *enables* automated exchange of information and transaction documentation between sites, businesses and countries.

So, if you can standardize technology and processes globally and significantly reduce transaction processing headcount, why bother with the cost and hassle of implementing SSOs with multicountry SSCs in them? Why not keep the current structure and implement a 'virtual SSO' with the following features:

- Staff are not consolidated but remain in existing and dispersed locations.

- A single 'virtual' shared services leader has responsibility for all functions and people wherever they may physically be.

- Systems and processes are standardized across the organization.

Based on this view, 'virtual' means:

- only the 'organization' will be virtual

- there will still be (automated but) real processes

- you will still need (possibly few but) real people.

Clearly, the above virtual solution would have some advantages:

- No staff upheaval – staff remain in existing locations until processes are automated.

- No requirement to find a site and build a physical SSC and then close later.

- No loss of knowledge built up with existing staff.

- No problems with obtaining local language skills.

- No cost and effort of hiring and training staff for the SSC.

However, to implement it, there also would be some prerequisites:

- clearly defined processes and responsibilities

- highly developed and secure IT structure.

Even if the above prerequisites could be fulfilled, the virtual solution has some issues to solve:

- Standard technology does not always lead to standard processes. There is widely spread misbelief that a process equals the system. In reality, a process is much more. It also includes interactions outside the system.

- Difficulty of implementing and maintaining different processes in several sites is a huge issue. To keep a process on one defined standardized level over time is quite difficult, and would be very difficult if not impossible in a virtual environment. In the best-case scenario, it would be costly.

- The remaining F&A management in country will experience poor spans of control because of virtual set-up. Compared with physical SSCs, this is a big negative, as the span of control is higher in an SSO.

- There would be a high cost to maintain finance management in all countries. Many financial benefits come from the reduction of top and middle management, not just from optimization of data-entry clerks.

- There will be no wage arbitrage, as the local cost structure is not changed.

- There will be a difficulty in sharing and implementing best-practice ideas in several sites, as every idea needs to be discussed and explained several times and even in positive case implementation costs will be high.

- There would be a difficulty in achieving service culture in existing local sites because old back-office culture is based mainly on existing personnel and will remain in place.

In 2001, 19% of companies claimed to have a virtual SSO (according to akris). This is presumably based on quite a number of companies claiming to have an SSO or calling their back-office organization shared services or similar, even though in reality they just were not willing or able to consolidate. Newer research does not provide answers on this figure. Possibly the disbelief in the consolidation benefits have died out.

In terms of benefits, the virtual solution can deliver some of the benefits but not all of them, as shown in Figure 65.

Although much benefit can be reached by process optimization and IT standardization, the consolidation element still counts for 25–50% of the total benefits available. Also, keeping standardization inside such a distributed environment is

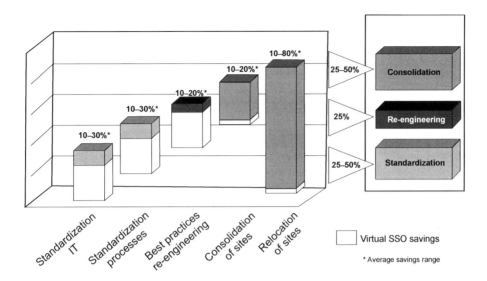

Figure 65   Sources for savings in virtual SSO

difficult and cost intensive. Hence, virtual SSOs of the kind that are discussed today are, at best, a step in the right direction. At worst, they are an alibi to avoid tapping into the benefits available.

Assuming the best case and the right intentions, the virtual solution would have the following success criteria:

- Stable foundation:
  - clear organizational set-up with clear (even if multiple and not necessarily local) reporting lines. A matrix is complex as such and needs clarity in implementation to have a chance
  - standardized and very clear and well-documented processes
  - comprehensive rules and regulations (policies and procedures) including manuals.

- Stable and advanced IT platform:
  - standardized IT on one enterprise application
  - advanced IT tools supporting workflow and paperless processes
  - efficient IT network management and maintenance.

- Social network with skilled personnel:
  - extensive training, coaching and mentoring
  - social activities to compensate for lack of head-to-head interaction
  - local coordination for site issues (working environment, HR issues, facility, insurance, contacts and so on).

The social component is often heavily underestimated. Think about teams put together for project work, journalists travelling around the world and only tied to their organization by a loose network, and similar jobs. Not having an office to go to and to meet colleagues in must be compensated for in the long term, otherwise the solution will not work. This will cost money and needs to be built into the comparison equation.

So, as a conclusion on virtual SSOs, even if we assume that they would be used with care and the right intentions, the conclusion would have to be that physical SSOs still make sense.

- First build physical SSCs:
  - facilitates simplification, standardization and optimization (SSO)
  - facilitates move to 'lights-out' processing
  - enlarges scope to build IBCs.

- Then make transactional SSCs redundant:
  - through continuous technological enhancements and process improvements turn lights out on low-value transactional work
  - arrive at virtual future.

Virtual SSO solutions can be used to support the physical SSO solutions and as means to get to the future state.

References and Information Sources

ACCA: *ACCA Research Report No. 79. Financial Shared Services Centers*, Martin
                Fahey, 2002

akris: akris.com *Shared Services Study*, 2001

ANSR: Answerthink Inc.

ANSR EU: Answerthink Europe GmbH

Collum: Hugh Collum, CFO SmithKline Beecham, Shared Services Presentation,
                2000

JBS: Commentary in *Journal of Business Strategy*, 2002

McMillan: Cary D. McMillan, Executive Vice President Sara Lee Corporation,
                Shared Services Presentation, 2001

Smith: Adam Smith, *An Inquiry into the Nature and Causes of the Wealth of
                Nations*, first published 1776

THG: The Hackett Group

Where not specified, the source is Answerthink and The Hackett Group.

Index

About the Author

Tom Olavi Bangemann is Senior Director at Answerthink and the European Practice Leader. Tom has over ten years' experience in accounting and consulting and has helped clients on over 25 shared service projects, which included all phases of the shared services lifecycle, a range of different industries, countries and company sizes, the internal shared services choice as well as outsourcing to a BPO. Tom has been publishing articles on shared service topics for the past five years and appears regularly as an acknowledged expert in chairman roles and speaks at approximately five to eight shared service-related conferences each year. Tom is married to Kristina Marie and they have a son called Ben.

ABOUT ANSWERTHINK

Answerthink[SM] (www.answerthink.com and www.answerthink.de) is a leading business and technology consulting firm that enables companies to achieve world-class business performance. By leveraging the comprehensive database of The Hackett Group, the world's leading repository of enterprise best-practice metrics and business process knowledge, Answerthink's business and technology solutions help clients significantly improve performance and maximize returns on technology investments. Answerthink's capabilities include benchmarking, business transformation, business applications, technology integration and offshore application maintenance and support. Founded in 1997, Answerthink has offices in 11 cities throughout the United States and in Europe.

ABOUT THE HACKETT GROUP

The Hackett Group, an Answerthink company, provides empirically based advice and best-practices research to executives seeking to drive world-class performance in areas such as finance, IT, human resources and procurement. Hackett's benchmarks and its confidential, on-demand, membership-based research and advisory services are supported by a regularly updated database of best practices in processes, technology and organization in use by over 2000 clients around the globe. This unparalleled information repository allows Hackett analysts to provide insight, analysis and recommendations with a level of integrity and authority available nowhere else. At the time of writing, Hackett clients comprise 97% of the Dow Jones Industrials, 81% of the Fortune 100 and 88% of the Dow Jones Global Titans Index.

Hackett serves European clients through regional offices in Eschborn at Frankfurt am Main and in London.